RAPE AND THE BIBLE

RAPE AND THE BIBLE

by

ALTON MEYER WINTERS

ISBN: 1-58820-325-5

This book is printed on acid free paper.

1stBooks - rev. 11/29/00

TABLE OF CONTENTS

PREFACE

The language and style of most Bible translations are appalling. The breathless piety, the blushing euphemisms, the archaic language; none of these is characteristic of the original text. Therefor, the vast majority of translations is false. In addition there are out and out misinterpretations in almost all translations. The author has a background as a professional translator of Hebrew. In this work, all the Bible translations are his own, and he takes responsibility for them. However, whenever the translation here differs in substance from published translations, that fact will be pointed out and the differences clarified in the text and the notes.

No translation from one language to another can be genuinely true. Even in the simplest things, sometimes, when one can accurately translate the words, the culture creates a gap that is impossible to cross. Take the easiest kind of word, "dog," for example. We think that everyone everywhere knows what a dog is. Yet there were no dogs in the new world until the coming of the Europeans. But still, we insist, everyone today knows what a dog is. At least here, in this kind of thing, there is certainly an area where the translator can do no wrong. 'Chien' means dog in French, as does 'kalb' in Arabic; and Chinese has a word which we are not going to bother to look up. But if a translator thinks he has no problem just because he knows the word, he or she is in for trouble. 'Chien', 'kalb', and that Chinese word, whatever it may be, might mean the same animal as the English word dog. But there the clarity ends. The Frenchman sees that animal as an accessory to style. The Arab puts the dog at the very bottom of his list. He might bring a sheep into his house, but never a dog. The dog is something to kick or throw a stone at. For the

Chinese, the dog is an item of diet. We all know the disgusting story of the lady who leaves her pet poodle in the care of the waiter at the restaurant in Hong Kong. Translating the word dog back and forth among those languages may be quite precise. But it is no translation. You, the translator, might add a note explaining the connotation of the concept "dog" in English. The Englishman at his fireside or shooting in his field or patting his faithful old friend would be some of the items in your note. The problem now, however, would be that no one would read your translation. After all, everyone knows what a dog is.

If the simplest things can prove troublesome in the translation of modern languages, the difficulty is multiplied, more truthfully, it increases exponentially, when we have to deal with ancient languages and the cultures in which they are current? If uncomplicated concrete objects and animals can be stumbling blocks, what can we say of ideas and abstractions? Still, as translators, we can only do our prayerful best.

While there is no pretense that the present work is scholarly in a technical sense, we hope not to offend scholars too much by our methods. If we offend them, or anyone else, by our conclusions, so be it. We have kept the notes to a minimum, and the style as simple and uncluttered as we know how.

Whenever transliterations of Hebrew occur, they are given in simple phonetic form. Those who know Hebrew will manage to understand the word that is transliterated. For those who do not know Hebrew, the transliteration does not make any difference anyhow. So-called scientific transliteration systems make no sense for this kind of book.

B.C. and A.D. are used to designate dates throughout the book, despite the fact that we know they offend many Jewish readers. These abbreviations are, after all, the norm when discussing history in our culture. Many non-Jews have trouble understanding the alternative symbols. We can simply clear our minds of the theological implications of the words and expressions we use in everyday practice. The Englishman says “by Jove” without feeling that he is betraying his religion. We call one of the days of the week Wednesday without thinking, every time we use the word, that it is Woden’s day.

INTRODUCTION

Rape is a constant fear for every woman, of almost any age, on the face of our planet. It is true that, like the rest of our fears, the fear of rape is not always at the top of a woman's conscious mind. Certainly, most men are not rapists, not even potentially or latently. But enough of them are that a woman knows the problem exists. There are times and situations when she can virtually forget about it. There are other situations when it crosses her mind. Tragically, there are moments when it becomes a present terror. But whatever the status may be at any particular time, the fear of rape is always there at some level of awareness. It is not simply that rape is mentioned constantly in the news media. Rape is there in all our cultural and artistic expressions. While it is relieved by many other themes, it comes up often enough that we cannot forget it. But that is still not the real point. News reports and cultural products are effects, not primary causes. The dread of sexual violence has shaped much of our civilization. The manners, mores, and customs of our social life would be very different if this dread did not loom forever in the background. Our education, formal and otherwise, shows the influence of this fact of life. Our legal system, in its deepest roots, as we shall see, has to take the reality of sexual assault into consideration.

Any element having that prominent a character in human culture is bound to show up in the political arena. Whether in the campaign for sheriff next November in our county or as British propaganda during World War I, or in the white supremacy speeches of a few years back, or throughout the Nazi racist hostilities against the Jews; the spector of rape refuses to be exorcised. We will see that the editors of the Bible decided to include the loathsome subject of rape mainly, perhaps solely, for political reasons.

This is a book about the Bible. By the way, when we use the term Bible, throughout this book, we mean what Christians call the Old Testament. A better name for it is the Hebrew Bible, even though a small part of is written in another language, Aramaic. The author is a life-long student of the Bible and its languages. If we make an attempt to characterize the Bible and its importance, that might become a book in itself. But briefly, the Bible is the most influential book ever written. It is more responsible for the values of our civilization than any other work. The Bible is not just the source for religions. It is a human work of great depth. There is probably no other product of the mind that displays as profound an understanding of human nature and the human condition as does the Bible. If any creation of human efforts deserves to be called divinely inspired, this is it.

But scripture is also a historical source of the most important kind. The miracles reported in the Bible plus the heavy theologizing that is almost universally present in scripture are uplifting to the believer. But they often put off the reader, student, or scholar who comes to the Bible with scientific training. It is easy for us to miss the plain fact that when scripture speaks of time and place and the basic shape of events, it has been shown to be almost invariably accurate. The Bible merits credibility as a source of history.

When it comes to the question of attitude toward the Bible, there are many widely divergent groups. We will not have named them all if we point to the skeptics and the cynics, the critics and the scientists, the searchers and the believers, the agnostics and the questioners. There are also fundamentalists of a number of religious orientations. This writer partakes of the characteristics of a little bit of many of those categories. But scientist-critic is probably the closest description of the approach used in this work. We are aware that there are many who regard the Bible as the unerring and perfect word of God. We can only respect the faith that lies behind such conviction. We have no desire to offend anyone who looks upon scripture in this way. We have no wish to undermine or destroy the beliefs of others. But, to us, the clear truth is that the internal evidence in the Bible itself shouts out the fact that the Bible is a human document. It reflects the philosophies, sciences, social views, and mores of the various times in which its parts were written.

The first mistake that most people make is in regarding the Bible as a book, as one book. It is an anthology that preserves the whole literature of a civilization. Its foundation documents were compiled under terrible pressure. Israel was destroyed by the enemy. The Babylonians overwhelmed the capital in 586 B.C. The city of Jerusalem and the precious Temple it contained were utterly laid waste. There had been thousands and thousands of casualties in the fighting. Nearly all of the survivors were taken away into exile. Most peoples in antiquity would have given up at that point. It was a common concept in those times that when nations fought on the battleground, their gods clashed on high. If your side lost the fight, then, you had to assume that your gods were also beaten. Obviously, those deities were no longer of any value to you. Who needs weak gods? Regularly, in the ancient world, defeated people adopted the religion of their conquerors. The Jewish religion, the prophetic burden in particular, conveyed a different message. It spoke of a universal Creator unbound by nation, place, or time. Judaism made it possible for Israel to survive. Scripture, the prophets and the book of Deuteronomy especially, made it clear that Jerusalem was lost not because of

Yahveh's weakness but due to Israel's sins. The Jews survived because they accepted responsibility for their failures and did not put the blame on God. The editors put together an anthology of the sacred Torah, the basic law codes, some of the most important prophetic pronouncements, vital historic records, and inspiring writings during and after the crisis of 586 B.C. This anthology, with later additions, became our Bible. It carried many messages. It taught national pride and the meaning of history. It expounded morality and presented a law to live by. But most of all, it was a work with a hero, God. All of its human heroes were real people with faults and flaws. Moses was a murderer who ran away rather than face the music. Jacob was a timid man, shrewd and deceptive. David was a murderer and adulterer. There are no perfect little plaster saints in the Hebrew Bible. They are all sinners, like us. That, in itself is inspiring. If those religious geniuses behaved that way sometimes, there is hope for the rest of us.

But the anthology has a hero. God is mover of history, master of the universe, purposeful creator, merciful source of grace, and demanding lawgiver. All powerful, He allowed the destruction of Jerusalem as punishment for Israel's failure to live by the Torah, establish a just social order, and worship Him alone. But the punishment is a sign of His mercy and grace. When the time of punishment is over, He will forgive. A small remnant can then return from exile to rebuild the state, the city, and the Temple.

We view the Bible as a collection of human documents. For some people, that seems to mean that we are trying to downgrade the Bible or deny God's role in it. But frankly, let us ask, which Bible is more uplifting? If the scriptures were dictated word by word to human stenographers, what would be so good about that? Does God want the credit of authorship? Does God want to control the copyright? If our Creator desired us to be a lot of puppets at the end of His strings, would He have made us free? If He did dictate the book would it teach pre-natal influence, speak of four legged grasshoppers, or calculate the value of pi as three?

The fact that this is a work of human origin does not put the Bible down. The truly exalting, thrilling thing is that people could produce such a lofty piece of writing. It comes out of the rough and tumble of real life. It addresses our condition as no other book can. If it shows the fingerprints of humanity on every page, it testifies also to the presence of the hand of God in every word. This kind of philosophy of the Bible teaches us the most important lesson that mankind needs to learn. We have the power to raise ourselves up out of the mud if we turn our gaze on the light from above and reach out toward it.

We feminists are never satisfied with any point of view about anything unless it grants total equality to women. We are right. We should not compromise in matters of principle. But, unfortunately, we do not find this equality anywhere ever in all the world's literature. The Bible is no exception. It is a mixed bag. Scripture is ambivalent on the subject. On the one hand, the wives of the patriarchs are powerful personalities. Their contribution to the molding of the future nation is indispensable. Miriam has an essential part to play in the salvation of the slaves in Egypt, the exodus could not take place without her courageous actions. Deborah comes to the rescue of the people of Israel at one of the most crucial moments in history, and no one else, certainly no man, could have duplicated her leadership role. The thirty-first chapter of Proverbs dwells on the merits of the outstanding woman. She is a fountain of energy, a charitable virtuosa, a talented real estate dealer; and not just a loyal wife, mother, and domestic saint. Yet, on the other hand, the books of Amos and Isaiah both contain sharp, specific denunciations of women. Females are singled out because they are, in the opinions of these two monumental prophets, demanding and sinful, distracting and beguiling, vain and excessively bejeweled. When caught eating the forbidden fruit, Adam blames it all on God for giving him Eve. You can multiply examples on the positive side and also find some more on the negative. What you cannot find is the tiniest hint of a breath of tolerance for rape. It is never justified. It is never the woman's fault. It is always punishable. There are very few references to rape in scripture. But each of them is very important. It is important to us because we need to understand the values of the most influential book in the world. It was important at the time it was written because it helped shape the political and legal systems of ancient Israel. Every single rape episode in scripture was included because of its political significance. This, as we will show, is the case in the story of the rape of Dinah, the vicious and murderous gang rape at Gibeah, and the incestuous sexual assault perpetrated by Amnon against Tamar. The Bible editors even had political motives in introducing the story of the false rape accusation leveled against Joseph.

The political issues involved in these several incidents were, as we will see, supremacy among the tribes of Israel, the problem of whether or not ancient Israel needed a human king, and the succession to the throne of David's empire. There were laws in Israel against rape from the earliest times. In fact, the Biblical laws on this and other subjects drew upon a long legal tradition, already ancient at the beginning of the Biblical period. This heritage was honored and understood throughout the entire Middle East. Legal codes from ancient Mesopotamia influenced the shaping of the rape laws in the Bible. Hittite law also shows some relationship to the provisions in the Torah on rape and other questions.

To have a law is one thing. To enforce it is often quite another. By default, in times of chaos when the law is unenforced, people take matters into their own hands. The blood redeemer sets out on a vendetta. But acts of vengeance do not end violence, they perpetuate it. This is a reality which the Bible recognizes clearly. It is a principle reason that the editors of scripture included subject matter which would otherwise have been passed over.

It is too much to hope than an understanding of the past will lead us to solve our problems in the present. Specifically, in the area of rape we have not improved things in thousands of years. If anything, we have moved in the wrong direction. We cannot expect a book, not even the Bible, to change the ways of human nature. Yet, what we do have in scripture is a warning. If we do not confront crime with just and severe punishment, our entire social structure will be undermined. Rape especially, is such a devastating kind of outrage that it eventually brings about uncontrollable emotional responses. The message of history, as conveyed in scripture, is that we had better do something about this crime and other unacceptable behavior.

Strict law enforcement is a necessity. It is not just that police efficiency should be maximized in rape cases. Police attitudes need to be sharpened. Policemen, in the past, have not always taken rape as the deadly serious matter it is. They have not always used a sufficiently sensitive approach to the victim. Too often, the closer the rapist is in race, religion, language, and national origin to the cops; the more lightly his crime has been regarded.

Education at the home and school levels must be more energetic. Some boys and men seem to have trouble seeing women as persons. This may be something that fathers can teach their sons, more by example than by lecture. In earlier generations, girls were frequently made to feel that sex in general, and rape in particular, was not subject matter for open discussion. Too often, when women were victimized, they kept quiet about it. Perhaps, sometimes, they even felt that the rape might have been their own fault. Worst of all, they seemed sometimes to have felt that rapes took place more or less in the normal course of things! At any rate, they could only suffer more, and bring shame on their families, if they made public what had happened to them. These feelings seem to persist, to some extent, even in our day. The education of girls, at home and in formal teaching situations, should dispel any misconceptions in this direction. Raise your voice. With a man's conditioning and instincts we are tempted to give masculine advice: Scream out -- before, during, and after the outrage. But in the event, each woman must be the best judge of how to handle her own confrontation. A woman must weigh the risks when confronted by a violent man. If he is armed with a knife or gun or other lethal weapon, she is the only one who has the right to determine how to conduct herself. For her, at that moment, rape is strictly an individual problem.

More is at stake, however, for the rest of us, than justice and legal remedy for individuals. Social tranquility suffers when we do not accomplish the arrest, conviction, and strict punishment of criminals in general. And rapists are in a special category. Our study of the Bible shows exactly the political character of the threat that rape poses. Men and women, society at large, would do well to pay attention to the ancient warning.

Chapter I:
WHY IS THERE SO MUCH SEX IN THE BIBLE?

Many people, especially those who have never read the Bible, have the idea that it is a nice, prim little book. They think that the Bible was written by saints who intended it to be studied only by respectable, God-fearing, religious folk. Nothing could be further from the truth on all scores. It was written by spiritual geniuses who were also sinners. They intended it to be read by and to the masses of men and women. The writers were interested in the washed and the unwashed, the rich and the poor, the blue stockings and the high livers.

Nowhere in scripture is sex brought in just to capture attention or pander to low tastes. But when they are part of the historical account, or when they serve the writers' purposes, sexual matters are openly and unblushingly discussed. Not many cases of rape are reported in the sacred literature. But our thesis is that, when they do occur, the reasons for presenting them are invariably political. Where sexual violence was turned to political ends or could be used to make a political point, the Biblical authors did not hesitate to make use of them. In this, the writers no doubt served their tribal or national leaders faithfully.

Sexuality as a motif pervades the contents of the thirty-fourth through the thirty-ninth chapters of the book of Genesis. If we are to understand the two episodes in which rape is the central theme, we must be aware of this larger canvas. We have to ask ourselves why sexual matters are so prominent as a background for those two episodes.

What appears to be happening in these chapters is the elimination of all competition for Joseph's claim to leadership in Israel. Only Judah emerges relatively unscathed. All of Joseph's other brothers who are sons of the legitimate wives, Rachel and Leah, are disqualified. In each case their iniquities have something to do with sex, and it is against a sexual background that Joseph's moral superiority is made plain. It is this which leads to Joseph's brilliant career and makes it possible for him to save Israel in the time of world famine. It is this moral superiority which, in the minds of at least one group of Bible editors, entitles the Joseph tribes to the dominant position in later Israelite history.

Right in the midst of the whole process, in chapter thirty- five from the last part of verse twenty-two through verse twenty-four (Gen.35.22b-24), the editor of the book of Genesis chooses to insert a genealogy. Most Bible readers are bored by genealogical lists, the famous "begats." But the presence and position of this particular one should not be treated lightly. In its time, the political impact of this editorial maneuver was powerful. The sons of Jacob are listed by their mothers in order of seniority. Leah's sons are Reuben, Simeon, Levi, Judah, Issachar, and Zebulun. Rachel's sons are Joseph and Benjamin. If indeed power is the issue in these chapters, then obviously Benjamin is no threat, since he was born after Joseph. But what of Issachar and Zebulun? They are certainly older.

Genesis thirty-five reports that Judah found a mandrake and turned it over to his mother, Leah. The mandrake is an herb the root of which was thought to resemble the human form. Magical powers were ascribed to this root, especially its power to cure infertility and assure the birth of children, more particularly of sons. In Genesis thirty-five, the barren Rachel sees that Leah has obtained a mandrake. Rachel, yearning to have children, pleads with her sister, Leah, to give her the precious root. Leah does so, but drives a hard bargain. Leah has fallen out of favor with Jacob, their husband. Rachel was his first love, after all, and has become the favorite wife. Now Leah sees a chance to reclaim her former status, if only for a time. She insists she be ceded the right to sleep with their husband Jacob first. As a result of this arrangement, Issachar and Zebulun are born before Joseph. But most probably they are no threat in the succession to power because their very existence is due to the concession made to their mother by the mother of Joseph. It is interesting, by the way, to note the powerful status of the women at this early time. Jacob, who clearly prefers Rachel at this point in his life, has no choice but to recognize the bargain between his two wives and meekly accept Leah, at least temporarily, as partner in the marriage bed.

So much for Benjamin, Issachar, and Zebulun. They can never challenge Joseph for leadership. Dan, Naphtali, Gad, and Asher are sons of the concubines, Bilhah and Zilpah. They are out of the running from the start. But that still leaves Reuben, Simeon, Levi, and Judah who stand in the way of Joseph's dreams. They must be cut down to size to fulfill Joseph's ambitions, or the ambitions of the interests served by the editor who put these chapters in the form in which we have them. Reuben is gotten rid of in very short order. There is a terse notice, in the first part of the verse to which we referred before (Gen.35.22a), that takes care of him. "Reuben went and slept with Bilhah, his father's concubine, and Jacob heard." That is all we are told, and it is quite probable that this brief notice is all that the editor left us from a much longer and detailed account. It is not so hard to guess why the editor might have reduced such an account to a pithy sentence or two. The subject matter would probably have seemed very unsavory to the leaders and people of the time. Not that they would have objected to a juicy sexually colored tale. There are plenty of them in scripture, and they were as popular then as now. But this one, after all, concerns a skeleton in the family closet. The shorter and less conspicuous you can make it the better. Part of a verse in the middle of a paragraph buried in the heart of an obscure chapter and just before a genealogical table which most people skip would be fine. Still, it cannot be entirely omitted because it concerns an important development in the nation's history.

There is no doubt that Jacob remembered the event literally to his dying day. At the end of his life, Jacob-Israel offers a statement characterizing all his children. This is often spoken of as Jacob's "blessing." But the Bible does not use that term. Jacob himself says that he will tell his sons what will befall them in the future. His reference to Reuben naturally comes first. He pronounces these words (Gen.49.3-4):

> "Reuben, my oldest, you are my strength,
> The first of my virility; the best of my vigor and power.
> Unstable as water, rule not.
> For you usurped your father's bed.
> You defiled. He climbed up on my couch."

Reuben's adulterous act is bad enough on the face of it. Although Bilhah is not his mother, the deed still smacks somewhat of incest, of the violation of the family's very fabric. But what is not at first plain to modern readers is the fact that, in the context of the culture of Bible times, Reuben's crime also had a political character. The usurpation of the king's or chieftain's concubines is a revolutionary declaration. It is a way of saying that the old leader is finished, the new leader is the one who is man enough to seize the royal concubines. This is especially clear in the book of Second Samuel where Absalom, in his attempt to wrest power from his father, King David, "goes in to his father's concubines (2Sam.16.22)." Reuben, then, is probably not giving in to lust or falling in love or simply philandering in this affair with a much older woman. He is seeking to replace his father, the chief of the clan and founder of the nation of Israel. The very intent of usurpation, just as much as the sexual infraction itself, disqualifies Reuben for the position he covets.

The case against Simeon and Levi we shall leave till later. It is part of an event in which rape is an issue and therefor occupies an entire chapter of its own in this book.

Scripture preserves a detailed account of the attempt to reduce Judah in rank. In Genesis chapter thirty-eight, Judah leaves home and marries a Canaanite woman. We are not told her name, but the name of her father is Shua. She bears two sons, Er and Onan, in short order. Sometime later she has a third son, Shelah. The first two boys are not exactly the picture of virtue. Judah obtains a wife for Er by the name of Tamar. But Er dies soon after the marriage, before he is able to have any children. Of his death we are told only "Er, Judah's first-born, was evil in God's eyes, and God killed him (Gen.38.7)." Judah calls upon the second son, Onan, to step forward now and fulfill the levirate obligation for his dead brother. When a man died without male issue, the living brother had to marry the widow. Any son from such a union would then bear the name of the deceased. Onan appears to be ready to fulfill this duty. But he begrudges his brother the son who might be born. So Onan, scripture informs us, ejaculates on the ground when he has intercourse with Tamar. This displeases the Lord, so He kills Onan, too.

Now it is Shelah's turn. But Judah tells Tamar that Shelah is still too young to carry out the levirate assignment. He advises her to go home to her father's house for a while until Shelah is ready. Scripture, however, lets us know Judah's real motive. He fears that Shelah will suffer his brothers' fate. At any rate, Tamar does depart for home.

Next we are told that a very long time passes. Then Judah's wife, the daughter of Shua, dies. After mourning for her, he follows his shepherds during the season of shearing the sheep. They near Timna, where Tamar is languishing, and she hears that Judah is coming. Tamar knows that she has been deprived of her rights and decides to take action. She puts off her widow's garments, dons a veil and robe, and sits down near the wells at the entrance to Timna. The modern reader does not immediately understand. And even if some of our translators do comprehend the actions she takes, there is no way that they can convey the significance of this change of dress. But to an audience in Bible times it would be instantly clear that Tamar is acting the role of a prostitute. Judah passes by, and when he sees a woman with her face covered, he considers her a prostitute. He is no longer married, and the period of mourning for his wife is over. Judah is free to ask for her favors, and she wants to know what price he will pay. He offers to send a kid from the flock later. She demands a pledge which she can hold until she is paid, namely his seal, cord, and staff. He consents to give her these to assure payment. (For us this would be like giving someone your driver's license and credit cards.) They make love. Tamar never removes the veil, so Judah still has no idea who she is. Tamar is pregnant. When Judah sends one of his people with the kid for the woman, she cannot be found.

In a few months time, Tamar begins to show. Someone from Timna reports to Judah that his daughter-in-law has played the whore and is also with child. Judah's reaction is immediate and firm. The family's honor is at stake. He wastes no words but simply says (Gen.38.24): "Take her out and let her be burned." Now Tamar makes her next move. She sends the seal, cord, and staff to Judah, her father-in-law, telling him that she is pregnant by the man to whom these articles belong. She asks him to identify the person that would be. Judah's public reaction saves Tamar from judgement. He states (Gen.38.26): "She is more in the right than I am because I did not give her to Shelah." Scripture adds that he never touched her again. He also appears to accept as his own the twin sons that are born to Tamar.

"She is more in the right than I" says it all. Neither Judah nor Tamar behaves in a saintly fashion in this report. Judah has left home and married a Canaanite woman without his father's consent, nor would Jacob have given it if asked. Judah has had nothing but misery and grief from his first two sons, Er and Onan. He breaks the law in trying to protect the third son. Judah's wife dies, and he observes the period of mourning before having another woman. But when he finally becomes sexually active once again, he runs afoul of Tamar and faces the sharpest, or perhaps the second sharpest, test of his character in his whole life. He can deny Tamar easily. Who better than she, his relative, could have had the opportunity to steal his credentials? How could she have fallen into harlotry or adultery when all she had to do was ask him for Shelah, the third son, whose services she was entitled to? He would never have denied this request, although he might have forgotten his obligations for a time, etc. The people would have accepted excuses of this nature, and Tamar would have already been burned to death anyway. But Judah displays his moral strength at the crucial moment. He takes the burden of blame, for the most part, on himself. He makes the best of the situation that he possibly can.

Incidentally, this is not the first time that Judah plays a questionable role in a crucial family event. Chapter thirty-seven of Genesis includes the clash between Joseph and his brothers. The brothers decide to kill the obnoxious teenager who seeks to lord it over them. Reuben, however, is in favor of simply throwing Joseph into a cistern and leaving him there helpless rather than actually shedding his brother's blood. It is Judah who saves Joseph's life. He uses psychology on the others and gives them the idea of making some easy money while getting rid of the unwanted sibling. Thus Joseph is sold into slavery and taken away to Egypt. Here, Judah takes part in the move against his brother, he consents to the ruse by which the brothers convince their father, Jacob, that Joseph is dead; but he is solely responsible for preventing the murder. Perhaps, if we have to look for a reason for Judah to leave home and marry out of the clan, we have his motivation here. He could not bear to remain with his wicked brothers. He could not stand the ordeal of witnessing his father's continual grief. He was not up to telling the old man the truth and suffering the consequences. So he left.

Whoever edited these chapters in Genesis had the intention of showing Joseph's superiority, probably for political purposes. But another editor, with different political sympathies, was interested in promoting the image of Judah. Judah emerges from the process as a real human being with his good and bad sides. He becomes involved in problematic ethical situations, approaching immorality. But he does not actually commit either adultery or murder. If his behavior toward his father is inconsiderate, let us remember that Joseph, too, once he won his freedom and gained great power in Egypt, could have let his father know that he was still alive.

Now that we have some understanding of the reason that scripture preserves these sexually hued chapters, we are ready to move on to a consideration of the frightening trial which Joseph had to undergo. It is a nightmare that all men fear and many have had to live through.

But first let us not forget the two brothers who still stand in the way. Simeon and Levi block Joseph's path to hegemony. In chapter thirty-four of Genesis, the editor tapped an old tradition of a story charged with rape, passion, and violence to accomplish his purpose. We must consider that episode now.

Chapter II:
THE RAPE OF DINAH

The setting for the episode described in Genesis thirty-four is the central mountains of the land of Canaan. Jacob has returned from Syria to the country in which he was born. He had left with nothing more than his staff and a little pack. Now he has come back, decades later, as the head of a powerful clan with great wealth. He and his twelve sons and their people lead a pastoral life with enormous flocks and herds as their most important possessions. They have settled near the city of Shechem. It is a strongly walled town, the hub of commercial and agricultural life in this region. Shechem is occupied by a Horian population whom the Bible calls Hivites. These are non-Semitic people, and the men are, therefor, uncircumcised. Jacob has probably had many daughters by his two wives and two concubines, but we are told of only one, Dinah, the daughter of Leah. This Dinah is the central figure in our story.

She goes out one day to visit with some of the women of the land. The son of the ruler of the region, a young man by the name of Shechem sees her, grabs her, and rapes her.(1) At this point and indeed throughout the chapter we are not given much insight into the effect which this dreadful event has on the young inexperienced Dinah. The entire episode is as if seen solely through masculine eyes. The issues involved are men's concerns: power, desire, honor, blood, greed, and violence. We are first informed about the consequences of the act for the perpetrator, Shechem. His reaction is unexpected. He falls in love with the maiden he has raped and speaks to her of his emotions. We might expect some response on Dinah's part here, but there is not a word. It is just possible that the rapist is doing something that could have been expected. He may be acting within the framework of a common legal tradition that operated throughout the region. Of this, we will say more in chapter six. Perhaps we are to conclude that her silence is consent, a way of saying that if he wants to marry her she will accept and make the best of a bad situation. Or, it may be, that she keeps her tongue thinking: "Wait a bit, and my father and brothers will take care of you." We have no way of really knowing. Shechem would seem to have understood consent. For he now goes to his father, Hamor, to ask for help. Hamor is an interesting name, by the way. It means donkey or ass, and may be a derogatory distortion of some original name. Shechem requests his father to obtain Dinah as a bride. Shechem wants the woman he has raped to become his wife.

The text of the Bible never really makes it clear until the very end of the account, but Dinah remains in Shechem throughout the episode. Whether she is kept there against her will or not is another issue on which we are uninformed. Adding the acts of kidnapping and possible unlawful detention would compound the rapist's crime. It would also bring the situation home to us. Many thinkers today are concerned with the concept that rape, in addition to its criminal character, also constitutes a violation of the civil rights of the victim. A woman grants sexual favors purely as a matter of her own choice. Her body belongs to her alone. That means that violence and sexual assault are not only crimes of a felonious nature, they are, as well, acts that deprive the unwilling victim of her status as a citizen and a human being. It appears that this is not just a modern argument. Jacob and his sons have the point of view that a woman possesses inviolable status. When they characterize Shechem's assault as "something just not done in Israel," it is first and foremost this sort of deprival to which they refer.

The report of what has happened gets back to Jacob almost immediately. But the distraught father keeps silent. At the moment when Jacob learns of the event, his sons are all away tending the flocks. Word is sent to them, or in some manner they come to know of what has occurred. They return at almost the same time as Hamor, Shechem's father, arrives to speak with Jacob. The brothers come back in a high emotional state. Scripture tells us (Gen.34.7): "Jacob's sons came in from the field as soon as they heard. The men were very overwrought and angry because an outrage had been committed against Israel to lie with Jacob's daughter, something that is not done." The language here sounds a bit anachronistic to us. The question, of course, is the meaning of the word "Israel." If it refers to the individual, Jacob, then the sentence makes sense in context. It is simply a synonym for the name of the outraged father. It is the name which God gave Jacob after their mysterious wrestling match in Genesis thirty-two. However, if the appellation is meant to designate the extended family of Jacob, the clan, it would give us difficulty because that meaning would be very rare, or even unique for the period in question.(2) But if the name, Israel, is used here to designate the "people", Israel, we have something of a problem. Does the Israelite nation exist at this time? Technically, it does not. The clan is not to become tribes and the tribes a nation until the sojourn in Egypt. So if the name, Israel, refers to the people in this verse (Gen.34.7), the best we can make of it is that it is an adumbration. It foreshadows great and dire happenings that are to come. They are to be discussed in later chapters. The problem is not really so agonizing after all. We shall hear the sentiment and the language, "such is just not done in Israel," in circumstances that leave no doubt that the phrase has been inserted by an editor with political motivation.

Be that as it may, Hamor comes before Jacob and the brothers not just as the father of the love-smitten Shechem, but with larger interests. He proposes not only this one single marriage, but that the Jacob clan establish a regular relationship with the people of the area of Shechem. They should all marry one another freely. They should all live together. The land would be open for Jacob's people to settle and trade in unrestrictedly. There is little doubt that Hamor views the deed of his son as nothing more than minor mischief on the part of a rambunctious lad. But what is more, Hamor the chieftain sees this as the moment of opportunity. He has had a look at Jacob's flocks and herds and the substance of the wealth of Jacob and his sons. The tiff over an injured girl and some hurt pride constitutes a stroke of good fortune in Hamor's view. True, the concessions he is offering Jacob are of some value. But the city of Shechem and its chieftain will derive the greater benefit. Just think of the tax collecting possibilities alone if all these nomads can be induced to settle down. That is how Hamor sees it.

Now scripture gives us a glimpse of the viewpoint of the son. Shechem speaks to the humiliated father and the enraged brothers. "Show me your favor, and I will give you whatever you say. Make the marriage price as great as you like, and I will pay it, if you will just give me the girl as a wife (Gen.34.11-12)." Perhaps Shechem and his father are not actually so different from each other. Each of them is offering something of material value. The father draws a picture of equal citizenship and economic opportunity. The son is willing to let Dinah's family name the price, a sure way to lose any negotiations that might follow.

But neither father nor son has read the hearts of the men whom he is addressing. Jacob has been known from childhood for his shrewdness and his ability to outcheat those who would cheat him. It seems that his sons are apples that have not fallen far from the tree. The Bible reader can only imagine the circle of straight faces and innocent looking eyes that are turned on the lovesick rapist and his rapacious sire.

The sons of Jacob now take over the proceedings. Scripture specifically informs us (Gen.34.13) that it is with deceit that they make their counter proposal to Hamor and Shechem. The Bible leaves us with no doubt that this approach is justified, because their sister has been defiled. They will not deal with the rapist on his own level. Jacob's sons, we are not told exactly who does the talking for them, base their position on what we would call religion (they had no word for it). They say that they cannot allow their sister to be married to an uncircumcised man. But if all the men of Shechem will be circumcised, and there is a commitment that in future all male children will be purified in this manner; then there can be unhindered intermarriage between the two groups. They can become a single nation. If not, the Israelites will take their leave (Gen.34.13-17).

What is happening here is, of course, that the brothers of Dinah are responding to Hamor's offer. If the issue were solely the marriage of their sister to the man, Shechem, then the circumcision of that one person might be sufficient. But Hamor has proposed the union of the two peoples and has dangled some supposed material advantages in front of Jacob and his sons. They give the appearance of falling for his proposition. They also add a definite threat. If Hamor and his people do not comply, Jacob and his people will take their leave. Hamor sees all that wealth leaving his realm. Shechem sees his bride disappearing. They both react quickly. Shechem, the smitten son, is circumcised immediately. Hamor goes back to town where he and the youngster now take on the task of winning the agreement of the men of the city of Shechem to a little operation.

They present two arguments. First, here is Shechem, the most distinguished citizen of the city whose name he bears. He has already undergone the ordeal, are you man enough to join him? Or, alternatively, here is Shechem, etc., who has already benefited from this healthful, cleansing operation that makes sex better; don't postpone it! Or, alternatively, he's done it, there's nothing to it. We cannot be sure which drift is given this first argument. It was probably left to the men of the city to draw their own conclusions. But the motivation of the second line of reasoning is quite clear. It is greed. Hamor and his son state (Gen.34.21-23): "These people are being frank with us. They will live and trade in the country, and the land will be opened wide before them. We will take their women as wives and give ours to them. But only by this will those men consent to live with us as one nation: If every male among us is circumcised as they are. Will not their cattle and their property and all their animals be ours? If we just satisfy them, they will live with us." The men of Shechem are persuaded. All of them are circumcised.

Now the narration in Genesis moves to its climax. On the third day after the circumcision, while the people of the city are still in pain, Simeon and Levi, Jacob's sons and full brothers of Dinah, take up their swords. They move against the town with ease.(3) They kill every male. "They slew Hamor and his son Shechem at the edge of the sword, took Dinah from Shechem's house, and left (Gen34.26)." We may wonder about two men accomplishing a feat of such dimensions, even under very favorable circumstances. It is possible that by "Simeon and Levi" scripture means the two brothers and their followers, their servants, fighting men they retained, or the like. Still, it is remarkable what individuals or quite small groups can do in battle under the right conditions. The men of Shechem are perfect victims for a sudden, treacherous attack. They are still in pain, the

Bible tells us, from the operation. But even more important, they are congratulating themselves on the clever deal they have made with these rich but innocent Semites, the rubes (a word which probably comes from Reuben, by the way). The last thing that would have occurred to Hamor is that these country bumpkins are smarter or more cunning than he. Moreover, Hamor could never be brought to believe that the indignation shown by Jacob and his boys is genuine. He would not have taken it so seriously, why would they? There is a wide gap in values and standards between the two men and their groups. When scripture tells us that this is "something just not done in Israel," there is probably an implication that "this" may happen and be passed off as normal elsewhere; but we cannot tolerate it. And as for the son, Shechem, like all bullies everywhere and always, he is not much of a fighter to begin with. Even if he had been prepared for the attack, he would not have show much ability for violence against men.

The next phase of the episode (Gen.34.27-29) would not be a matter of pride to moderns. It would not be acceptable. But it is actually what happens after most battles even today. To the editor of the Bible it is entirely justifiable. The ancient Hebraic philosophy is that not just an individual, but an entire community has committed a crime. The whole city is guilty. The whole city is to be punished. "Jacob's sons came upon the casualties and plundered the city which "had defiled their sister." The repetition here of the reason for the conflict puts the Israelite side in the right beyond all doubt. The brothers of the ruined maiden proceed to take all the flocks, cattle, donkeys, and property in and around the town. They capture all the women and children and their property, along with all of the household goods. It seems that they even take the pagan idols, for in the very next chapter

(Gen.35.2ff.) Jacob forces his people to rid themselves of foreign gods.

At the conclusion of the episode, Jacob scolds Simeon and Levi. He finds fault with them, but not on the basis of principle. He fears that they have given him a noisome reputation that will bring other people of the land to unite against him and destroy him. Again, it seems, Israel senses that rape is not going to be taken seriously by the others. Jacob does not say that the deed of his two sons is unacceptable to him. His fears are based on his knowledge that it will not seem justifiable to others. But for Simeon and Levi the issue is clear beyond all practical considerations. They respond simply: "And should he have made our sister like a whore? (Gen.34.31)" (4)

We have emphasized the differences in values as to the illegitimacy of rape because that difference is stressed in the Bible. This is not the only passage where Israelites are saying that they have a harsher view against rape than other peoples do. Factually, it should be said that if there is a difference in values it is a matter of degree only, and perhaps not even that. All the Mediterranean societies of the time had strong feeling, traditions, and laws. Rape within a community would likely have been anathema almost everywhere. Rape of an outsider, as in the account we are considering, might be treated a little more leniently in some places.

Be that as it may, the historical actuality is not our main concern here. The important thing for our study is how the Israelites saw themselves and how they felt about the problem of rape. They viewed rape as a total abomination not to be tolerated under any circumstances and deserving of the severest punishment to be administered unhindered by the injured party, that is the male relatives of the dishonored girl. Not until the Deuteronomic code of law in the seventh century B.C. will we see rape handled calmly within the legal structure. If we grasp the formula that rape justifies violent vengeance, we will be prepared to understand the implication of the rapes reported in scripture. They all have social and political significance.

A question which generally comes up when we study the Bible as a human record of human events is the validity of the text. How old is the narrative reported in Genesis thirty-four? If political use is made of it in later times, and we shall see that that is indeed the case, is it not likely that it was really written in those later times? It could be involved in the attack on the Benjaminites, or the struggle between the tribe of Judah and the Joseph tribes (Ephraim and Menasseh) for power, or the quarrel of the right of succession among the sons of King David. Indeed, the partisans in one or all of those controversies may have referred back to the rape of Dinah and its consequences as support for their side of the cause in which they were interested. But none of that means that the passage is late or artificial or made up out of the whole cloth.

The character of Levi in this account is clear evidence of the early and valid composition of the piece. There is no anticipation here whatsoever that Levi is to be the progenitor of the priestly caste; of a special, landless, consecrated tribe whose role will be to serve God. In this chapter we encounter a secular Levi, a warrior and a candidate for the leadership among the clan's members. He has to be eliminated, just like the others, to establish Joseph's priority. Jacob's pronouncement upon them in his ancient blessing-prediction is almost like a condemnation. In fact it is a deathbed declaration of his own innocence (Gen.49.5-7):

> "Simeon and Levi are brothers.
> Their weapons are instruments of violence.
> My soul, enter not into their conspiracy!

My dignity is not part of their company.
For in their wrath they slew men.
They emasculated bulls willfully.
Cursed is their anger because it is fierce,
Their rage because it is hard.
I divide them in Jacob.
I disperse them throughout Israel."

Only the last phrase hints at the place Levi will have in the future nation. But the remainder of the statement is surely a denial of everything that would fit a man and his descendants for the priesthood. Compare Jacob's sentiments in Genesis with the characterization of the tribe of Levi in the book of Deuteronomy (Deut.33.8-11). There, in a passage that could have been written as late as 613 B.C., Levi emerges as the self-effacing priest officiating with his sacred accouterments, teaching law and justice to the people. The passages in Genesis predate any assumption as to the role of the Levites in a sanctified position in Israel. Not only is Levi separated from Simeon, his ancient partner in crime, in the deuteronomic statement; but Simeon is not even mentioned in the blessing of Moses, as Deuteronomy thirty-three is known. The authenticity of the account of Dinah's rape and the events that followed it is assured in its essentials. The prominence it is given in Genesis, as well as the length and detail afforded it, is due to its importance in the process of giving Joseph the honor of first position among his brothers. The sexual infractions of Reuben, Judah, Simeon, and Levi are now to be contrasted in scripture with the purity and moral superiority of the brother whom they have sold as a slave into Egypt.

Chapter III:
A MASCULINE NIGHTMARE

No rape occurs in the episode we are to consider next. Yet rape becomes the main theme as the ancient writers, men no doubt, contrast masculine virtue with feminine duplicity. The poet has said that a woman scorned has a fury beyond anything to be found in hell. It is a rage of hatred of which men are fearfully aware.

For men, the relationship between the sexes is a baffling puzzle. Young men often seem brash and forward. More mature men can appear to be very sure of themselves. But, for the most part, men of all ages, in their dealings with women, are like blind people groping their way through an endless maze on a foggy, moonless night. Boys and girls, men and women, husbands and wives can have long conversations that are outwardly full of meaning and continuity. Yet the men, though they sometimes appear to be attentive, seldom really listen; and the women seldom find a way to say what they would like to convey. The problem, in the judgement of this male writer, is more with the men than the women. It is not just that many man consider women to be less intelligent than themselves. It goes beyond the fact that a great number of men see women as talkative, gossipy, trivial, light-headed, and illogical. If a lot of men feel that women do not make sense, that is just the beginning of the problem. The essence of the difficulty is in men's self-image. We see ourselves as logical, strong, decisive, men-of-action, men-of-few-words.

That would all be harmless if it ended there. But the nub of the inter-sexual question, the source of its complexity, and the factor that creates the vast gap between the sexes is men's conviction that the women must also regard them in keeping with the male self-view. That self-image of the strong, logical male is so firmly established in men's minds that they believe it to be absolute incontrovertible truth.

Men never hear how women actually feel about them. Or, if they do, they do not listen. Women, when they talk to each other about men, deliver a quite different message. On occasion they may communicate it to the rare male they trust, one who is capable of seeing them first and foremost as persons, although even he has thoughts of sex not far below the surface of his mind. What is said when women get to give their true perception of males is a shock to men's minds and egos. Men are irrational and undependable. They are flighty and inconsistent. They are impractical dreamers who live in a world of fantasy most of the time. They have a poor grip on reality and are generally unpredictable. They are unlike women in the characteristics that count most in life. Women are more practical, more down-to-earth, more in contact with reality. Men are bogged down most of the time because they see things in terms of ideas. Men overlook the fact that what makes the world work is people. Masculine utopias and abstractions always fail because men do not understand that they have to be run by people. Men teach history or mathematics or whatever. Women teach people. This is the way a great many women see men and understand the differences between the sexes. Women might say that no woman would work twenty years to achieve success in business and then throw it all over to sail to Tahiti. Somewhere in that sentence the women would insert the phrase "for no reason at all."

If we are more or less right in the foregoing description, we have set the background for an understanding of the popularity of the theme we discuss in this chapter. We would like to comprehend, also, the 'reasons' for the difficulty of intersexual communication. Those reasons might be genetic, physiological, psychological, or due to early conditioning of boys and girls. Probably, they are a combination of some or all of those factors. But the reasons do not make that much difference for our purposes. Men are aware that they are supposed to take the prime initiative in sexual matters. Women are at least somewhat influenced by the concept that it is "ladylike" to wait to be asked. Men propose or proposition. Women accept or reject. (A lady makes the man feel secure even when she says "no.")

If only it were that simple. But we all know that it is not. A man smiles at a woman across the room. She turns her head away, folds her arms, and not only crosses her legs but slips the toe of the top leg behind the ankle of the bottom one. That man should know that it would be foolish to waste the energy involved in walking over to her. But if she turns away, studiously ignores him, chats with a girl friend as if the guy did not exist, and gives her hair a funny little toss -- well then.... Boys come to know and appreciate these signals. Men realize that the "response" signals often precede the approach. Males come to realize that the girl is picking out and signaling to the man she hopes will get the idea that he would like to make a move in her direction. Start running, perhaps the right guy will pursue.

But all of that is only the beginning. There are false signals. A girl might give out what appears to be the right gestures and not mean it. She may change her mind when she sees the boy up close. She may have second thoughts at any point after she gets to know him, even after intercourse, even after marriage. From the beginning, she could just be testing her powers or his susceptibility. Or she might just be teasing. Or he might just be teasing.

In sex relations there are areas of uncertainty that last much longer than we usually realize. Throughout the stages of getting acquainted on up to the levels of foreplay, either party may step back and decide to end the relationship. This may happen after the first experiences of sexual intercourse or, as we have said, even after marriage. Occasionally, it may also occur during the sex act itself. Witness the action of Er and Onan in the practice of coitus withdrawal.

The situation is further complicated by the physical nature of sex. Two very different bodies are to come together in a special, delicate, violent way. The preparation for the act is not nearly the same for each of the partners. The two of them are of unequal strength. The softness of the woman is exciting. The power of the man is attractive. Men get to feel that some women want them to exert a little force, want to have a bit of a fight over every button and zipper, want to be made to do things that they would be embarrassed to perform voluntarily. We men are astounded when we read something like the answer given by quite a few women to a survey question on what they find sexually appealing in a man: "He makes me do things I don't want to do." The average man's reaction: "How's that again?"

All of this tends to make some people, some men in particular, believe that rape is a fuzzy business. Some men are able to persuade themselves that there are many false rape charges, and that an act that looks as if it might have been rape was not quite as bad as it seems. Some men, and perhaps a few women too, have a system of gradations worked out in their own heads. Things that happen in a "normal" sex relationship can grade off into the kinky. Then, sometimes, they can become violent. Women may then convince themselves that they were raped. Or a woman may regret or be ashamed of a relationship, especially a one-night stand. She may justify it, perhaps even in her own mind, with the claim that she was assaulted. The girl may give a false signal, or the fellow may misinterpret her words or gestures. She may be dressed provocatively and act as if she were on the make. The boys may say, when they hear one of the gang charged by her: "Everybody knows that gal is a terrible tease." All of the above, and more, might account for rape charges that some people consider suspect.

Unfortunately, some of the men who think this way are cops and lawyers and judges. The world, the world of men above all, must come to acknowledge that there is no fine progression between consent and rape. There is a sharp, unmistakable distinction. Of course, sometimes very tragically, men are falsely accused of rape. A girl or woman may make such an accusation for various reasons. She may speak out of hostility, vengeance, whim, or, as we shall see, out of fear and frustration. But that does not change the basic fact that should govern our sex lives. A woman has the right to refuse a man at any point, no matter what she has said, no matter how she acted, no matter how she is dressed. Even if a couple has slept together before, even if they live together, even if they are husband and wife; sexual intercourse must be an act of mutual consent. There are no gradations. The smart girl and the wise woman realize that there are limits beyond which she should not tempt a man if she knows that she is not going to want to follow through. But, in principle, that is not the essence of the matter at all. She always has the right to determine the use of her own body. There are no shades of gray, it is a black and white situation. And when rape does occur, it is never the woman's fault, no matter what! She always has the right to refuse.

And so does he. The predatory female who takes the initiative must be prepared for that refusal. Wise women learn that there are also men who are teases. But it is much more difficult for women. Culturally, the men are attuned to accept refusal and go on with their lives. Women are much more likely to be hurt by a snub. There are multiple threats to the woman when her offer of sexual favors is declined. The man may talk. She may become the object of gossip and scorn. Other men can get the idea that she is a push-over and act accordingly. And what if she is married? She was looking for a discrete little affair. She was going to eat her cake and have him too. But what will happen now? If he talks, she can always deny it. But maybe, just maybe perhaps, she can shift the onus to him.

In the period before the formation of the Israelite kingdom under Saul, after his coronation as the first king, and during the reigns of David and Solomon; the struggle for supremacy between the northern and southern tribes of Israel was quite sharp. Judah was the dominant tribe throughout this time. But the chief northern rival was Ephraim. That tribe bore the name of one of Joseph's sons who had been adopted by Jacob (Gen.48.5, 8-22). Genesis makes it clear that Jacob's intent was to give Joseph a double portion over that of his brothers. There are to be two tribes descended from the two sons of Joseph, Ephraim and Manasseh.

The political reality behind the Bible's rearrangement of the family pecking order was the rivalry of Ephraim and Judah before and during the era of the United Kingdom. Editors representing the interests of the northern group redacted Genesis thirty-four through thirty-nine in such a way as to demonstrate Joseph's (and therefor Ephraim's) right to the position of leadership. Southerners, Judeans no doubt, drew from different traditions to redeem Judah and prove his worthiness. Thus they justified the rights of the Judeans, particularly the powerful empire builders David and Solomon, to rule Israel.

After Solomon's death, the United Kingdom of Israel ceased to exist. It was split between northern and southern forces and was never reunited. So the text of the Biblical chapters (Gen.34-39) we are considering was pretty much completed as we have it by the end of the tenth century B.C. Of course, there were probably deletions, like the great bulk of the account of Reuben usurping his father's concubines. But there would not have been many additions. As for alterations, they would have become less and less possible as the very text itself began to be considered sacred.

Having taken a look at the setting within which they put it, we can now consider the gem with which the editors meant to convince us of Joseph's worthiness.

It will be remembered that Joseph was put into an uncomfortable position at home. He was the first son of Rachel, Jacob's favorite wife. The father doted on this child and showered him with kindness. Scripture mentions most prominently the princely coat with which Jacob presents the lad. At seventeen years of age, Joseph has dreams which foretell his supremacy over the rest of the family. This makes him unpopular with his brothers. When the opportunity comes, they conspire to kill Joseph but, at Judah's prompting, sell him to a passing caravan instead.

In Genesis chapter thirty-nine, Joseph has been brought as a slave to Egypt. He has been bought by a high official of Pharaoh, a courtier by the name of Potiphar. But, even as a slave, Joseph rises rapidly. Scripture tells us that the Lord was with him, and he was a successful person. He seems to have begun as a household servant. That, in itself is testimony to the favorable first impression he must have made. Certainly, most slaves, foreigners especially, started out as field hands. But in Joseph's case, the master sees from the beginning that this Hebrew youngster has talent and is capable of getting things done well. In short order, Joseph becomes the chief steward of the household with control over the entire estate. The house and the fields prosper under Joseph's management. The master gives him unquestioned rule over everything except for the food eaten by Egyptians. That would have had to have been prepared in accordance with the strict and complicated Egyptian dietary regulations; and no outsider, however otherwise trusted, would have been allowed to have the upper hand in that. So here is this fine looking, well built young slave running things to perfection and enjoying the complete confidence of his owner. This is not exactly the fulfillment of Joseph's youthful dreams. However, it is not so bad for someone who was almost murdered a short time before by his own brothers. But nothing can go that well for very long.

The master's wife looks Joseph over and commands him to come to bed with her. He refuses. He tells her that the master has trusted him with all the property of the household and does not even check on him. "He is not greater in this house than I and has withheld nothing from me except for you because you are his wife. How could I do this great evil and sin against God? (Gen.39.9)" His protestations, however, do not stop this woman. She repeats her demand every day, but Joseph will not obey her. Until one day, when Joseph comes into the house to do his work, and there is no one else at home except for him and her, she grabs his clothing and orders him into her bed. Joseph flees the house, leaving the garment in her hands; and the woman screams rape. She summons the servants and shows them the evidence of Joseph's clothing. When her husband returns, she repeats the performance and turns part of the guilt back on him: "The Hebrew slave you brought us came to me to sport with me.(6) But when I raised my voice and cried out, he left his garment with me and ran outside. (Gen.39.17b)" The master loses his temper. But he deals with Joseph more leniently than Simeon and Levi did with Shechem. Potiphar has Joseph thrown into the royal prison.

In the contest between mistress and slave, we have to suppose that there is little doubt which one would have been believed. Even so, one wonders why Joseph makes no attempt whatsoever to defend himself against the false accusation. Does he, too, feel that it would be futile? Does he hold back a truthful account of what has happened in order to spare his master's feelings. Joseph has faced death before and kept silence, in the presence of his brothers. He must know, now, that the penalty for the crime of which he is accused is death. But perhaps he senses that the master will not go that far in punishing him. Does the master know his wife better than we realize? Does Joseph understand that fact? Or does scripture mean us to conclude that in both cases, now and with his brothers, Joseph had no fear of death because of his trust in God. His youthful dreams of greatness are so real to him, he is so certain that they are of divine origin, that he considers any apparent evil that befalls him to be nothing more than a test. He accepts these repeated threats of death without fear. He believes unswervingly in the destiny that has been promised him. Whether he is aware of it or not, that destiny, in the mind of the Biblical writer, includes more than success in life. It is to bring dominance over the tribes of the future nation of Israel. Ephraim, one of the tribes of Joseph, will deserve to dominate the nation ahead of the concubine-seizing Reuben, the treacherously murdering Simeon and Levi, or even the philandering but honest runaway Judah.

The Joseph temptation story has great appeal to us at multiple levels. There is the theme of Joseph's virtue in the face of seductive persuasion. There is also the age-old male fear of being confronted with the charge of rape, especially when one is an outsider of different language and race. In the Biblical account we sense that there may be a weak relationship between the husband and wife. She seems to have need for some extra-marital stimulation. He does not trust her completely, or he would have Joseph executed. At any rate, it is the stuff of which rip-roaring drama is made. At least it seems that way to us, and no doubt was so for the people who heard and read the story in Israel of old.

But not only in Israel. The story in one form or another pops up all over the ancient Mediterranean world. Its appeal is ubiquitous and timeless. An Egyptian version exists from the thirteenth century B.C. It shows basic similarity to the Bible narrative, but there are also significant differences. Anubis and Bata are full brothers. The latter, the younger brother, lives and works in the household of the former. Bata sleeps outside the main house, while Anubis occupies it with his wife. So the first important difference in this story is plain. The two men are more nearly equals than were Joseph and Potiphar as slave and master. What is not apparent to the modern, non-Egyptian reader is that there is a mythological element which has somehow intruded here. Anubis and Bata are ancient Egyptian god names.

The Egyptian account is much more discursive than the very terse Biblical story. We are told at length how long and hard Bata worked to earn his keep, how loyal he was to his older brother, and how careful he was to keep his life separate from the main household. He is also a big, powerful, handsome man: "Why, the strength of a god was in him."(5)

There is an extended description of the way in which the two brothers worked together harmoniously day after day in the fields. There is no hint that the management of the farm was turned over to Bata. Indeed, it is quite clear that he worked under the direction of his older brother,

Anubis. But one day they run out of seed, and the younger man is sent back to the house to obtain some. He collects a prodigious amount, some eleven bushels, and is prepared to carry it away to his brother in the field when the wife stops to talk with him. She sees how much he is carrying, and says: "'How much is it that is on your shoulder?' And he said to her: "Three sacks of emmer, two sacks of barley, five in all, that is on your (sic) shoulder.'" (Read "my shoulder.") "So he spoke to her. Then she talked with him, saying 'There is great strength in you! Now I see your energies every day' And she wanted to know him as one knows a man." She invites him into her bed and promises to make fine clothes for him. He becomes enraged and scolds her. He declares his respect for his older brother and asserts that she and her husband are like mother and father to him because they raised him. He warns her not to repeat her invitation and he will not tell anyone of it. He returns to Anubis with the load of grain and they work together the rest of the day as if nothing had happened. Bata still has some chores to do at the end of the day. But Anubis goes straight to the house.

Meanwhile, the unnamed wife is afraid. She is not sure that Bata will hold his tongue. Perhaps she feels that he will always have something over her. We must remember, also, that he has reminded her how much older she is than he. That is not always a sure way to gain a woman's affection and favor. She prepares the scene carefully. The text tells us that she "takes" fat and grease. Some earlier translations interpreted this to mean that she smeared the grease on her loins to give graphic support to the claim she is about to make. But Pritchard's understanding is that she swallows these substances to induce vomiting. A consideration would be that the accusation of attempted rape would be more advantageous to her than to pretend that the sex act was completed. This way she is merely assaulted rather than dishonored. In fact, the drift of the story supports the thought that the fat and grease were eaten. She tells her husband that it was Bata who issued the suggestive invitation and beat her when she refused. She asserts that she reminded the youth that she was like a mother, and Anubis a father, to him. She adds that if Anubis does not kill him, she will kill herself. She admonishes her husband not even to let Bata speak. After all, a man who attempts to rape his brother's wife is also bound to be a liar. He will say anything to escape punishment and hold on to the comfortable life he enjoys. She expresses the feeling that, if she is forced to accuse him directly, he will only repeat the crime in the future.

It will be recalled that Joseph had to resist temptation more than once, that the wife of Potiphar (also unnamed) did not resort to dramatic props and extreme behavior (in fact she uses sarcasm rather than hysteria), and does not recommend what the punishment should be. The only evidence that Potiphar's wife shows is Joseph's clothing. But these differences seem rather minor compared with the overall similarity in the two accounts. However, the variations in what happens next are significant.

Anubis loses his temper and sharpens his spear. He hides behind the stable door to kill Bata. But the first cow to enter warns the younger brother that his senior lies in wait to kill him. The cow tells him to run for it. Bata flees with Anubis in pursuit, and a long chase scene ensues. Bata prays for justice to the sun god, Re. The god opens a large body of water full of crocodiles between the two brothers, and Bata gets a chance to speak in his own defence. He pleads innocence (though in the course of the story he has never heard the accusation) and tells Anubis the truth about what happened. To prove the truth of his testimony, Bata cuts off his own phallus and dies. Anubis returns home, kills his wife, and mourns for his brother.

Despite the fact that the end of the account goes off so far afield from the Biblical narrative, the resemblance between them is unmistakable. How can we account for this? What is the relationship between Genesis and the Egyptian tale of the two brothers? It would be hard to convince us that there is no relationship whatsoever. Of course, it could be argued that we are dealing with a theme of universal interest, reflecting common experiences and shared fears. But the nearly identical elements in the two stories make it impossible to take such arguments too seriously.

So we consider the possibility that the author of one of these narratives copied from the other. Somehow, when Biblical accounts resemble those of other ancient Near Eastern cultures, it is almost always taken for granted that the Bible's version was copied from the other one. This is generally the case when Biblical critics discuss passages like the creation and the flood stories. The likelihood of the Assyrians, Babylonians, or Egyptians copying from the literature of Israel has not been given consideration. Yet the earliest extant versions of the Babylonian creation story, for example, are probably later that the time of the composition of Genesis chapters one and two. Here, in the case of the Joseph temptation - two brothers accounts, the Egyptian story is dated very definitely by Pritchard late in the thirteenth century B.C., long after Joseph would have lived. Thus, if there was copying, it could have been either way. Both stories have quite clearly evolved considerably from their originals. The Joseph narrative has been reduced to the terse elements necessary for the political purposes of the editor. The Egyptian account has been expanded very discursively for the entertainment of an audience. The questions of whether one copied the other and who copied whom cannot be definitely answered on the basis of the data now available.

Thus, we have to consider another possibility; that the two stories both derive from a general theme that was very well known and popular in the culture of the entire region throughout antiquity. In this way, both scripture and the Egyptian writer drew upon a beloved story that touched several nerves in the male listener. It rekindled a fear that many men feel strongly, the dread of facing a false rape charge. It expressed a deep distrust of women and their wiles, casting doubt on their truthfulness, honesty, loyalty, and dependability. All in all an emotional feast for the masculine psyche.

This is not to say that the Joseph record is fiction. The tradition of Joseph's strength in the face of seduction is too strong to be rejected out of hand. The place of the temptation account is too central to be dispensed with easily. The flow of the entire history of Joseph, and therefor of the whole body of Israelite history, would be interrupted without this passage. We can live with the idea that something that happened in Joseph's life came close to conforming with the general lines of a popular theme. There is nothing wrong with this from a literary point of view. Truth resembles fiction so often simply because good fiction is always based on true life.

Actually, there can be little doubt that the false accusation theme ran through the whole extent of ancient eastern Mediterranean culture. In the form of the Hippolytus legend, for example, it appears in the works of Euripides and Sophocles in classical Greece, and it pops up in Rome in the writings of Seneca. As late as the seventeenth century, Racine uses it in one of his best known plays. And a modern Italian writer has reworked the theme.

Hippolytus, in Greek legend, was the son of an Amazon named either Antiope or Hyppolyte. Hippolytus was the illegitimate child of Theseus, and the father had probably raped the Amazon mother. Hippolytus grows up in the land where Theseus is king, Troezen. He is a great and powerful man, handsome, and a renowned hunter. Phaedra, the wife of Theseus, is attracted to the lad. During her husband's absence, she attempts to entice him, but Hippolytus refuses. Scorned and consumed by fear and hatred, Phaedra kills herself. She leaves a note claiming that her stepson raped her, and she can no longer face life. Theseus comes home just in time to find his wife's body and the words she has written. He will not allow Hippolytus the opportunity to clear his name. Theseus condemns the young man to death, and the sentence is carried out (possibly by tearing him apart with horses, the sense in which the ancient Greeks understood the name, Hippolytus). It is, no doubt, to be taken for granted that he is resurrected as a god, possibly brought back to life by Asclepius.

From early times, Hippolytus was worshipped at Troezen as a god and hero. It was customary for brides to offer a lock of hair at his shrine. Hippolytus was also remembered as a great athlete. In addition to the temple, there was a gymnasium dedicated in his honor. In Athens and Sparta also, tribute was paid to the god-hero. The legend and its message were popular in the ancient Greek world, and in classical times the story was recast many times in Greek and Latin literature. Sophocles wrote a play about Hippolytus, but only the merest fragments survive. Euripides composed two plays on the theme of the legend, and it influences other works that he created. Euripides first "Hippolytus" was severely criticized as morally objectionable. This may have been due to the fact, among other elements in the work, that there was a scene in which Phaedra declares her true love for Hippolytus in a face to face meeting. The classical Greek audience could understand lust and the workings of fate. Perhaps it was not ready to stomach a love that would pretend to be pure although outside of marriage. Euripides second effort written in 428 B.C., however, became one of the most popular dramas of its time. It remains an outstanding work of world literature. The second Hippolytus is really a story of the struggle between two goddesses. Hippolytus is a thoroughgoing woman hater. He not only rebuffs Aphrodite when it is suggested that he should have a love life, he insults the goddess very bluntly. Although he is the favorite of Artemis, goddess of the hunt, she cannot protect her votary from the wrath of the love goddess. It is Aphrodite who decides on the doom of Hippolytus. She puts the lust for him into the heart of Phaedra. She drives Phaedra on and on to the final deed and to the posthumous denunciation that leads to his death.

In Euripides, it is the fatal flaws in Hippolytus's character that bring about the catastrophe. He is disrespectful to a goddess. He is a misogynist. But much worse, he is virtuous to a fault. He deserts the golden mean between weakness and strength, love and conflict, domesticity and hunting, Aphrodite and Artemis. He is one-sided and proud. He never stops congratulating himself on his own perfection. From word one, he is riding for a fall. Phaedra, too, is guilty because she cannot find forces in her life to balance the influence of Aphrodite. And, likewise, Theseus is culpable in that he refuses to give his son a hearing. It seems likely that the Greeks of classical time understood clearly that Theseus was acting not only out of grief and anger. He had concern, as well, for his throne. For, if Hippolytus were reaching for possession of the queen, he was also trying to obtain the ultimate power in the kingdom. But we are being too Biblical with all this analysis. Actually, in the Greek mind, no one is innocent or guilty. Everything is a matter of fate. Human destiny is determined by the gods. Every person has a fateful flaw that casts the die. All the characters in the drama, all men and women, are helplessly lost in the clutches of fate. Though the story is recognizably close to the Biblical account, the values and world views of the two are poles apart. Our modern values are different, too. If we were writing the story, Phaedra would threaten to kill herself to save her honor and prevent the disgrace of her children, Theseus would regret having acted unjustly in a moment of anger, and Hippolytus would only seem to die. He would go from place to place trying to improve life for all the citizens, but he would run into trouble constantly because he was too good to be true. What a series it would make. In Seneca and Racine, Hippolytus is no longer the main character. They both concentrate on Phaedra. The classical Roman playwright presents us with a Phaedra who is a more normal person than the wild character she is in Euripides. She is simply a vile villain who acts out of frustration and anger. More than a thousand years later, the French dramatist softens her villainy by showing her sense of guilt and sorrow for what she is about to make happen. Racine's Phaedra has also had an illicit love affair with another man, Aricie. The attraction of the theme and story appears to be endless. It inspired the plot line of two of Euripides's other plays, "Bellerephon and Stheneboa" as well as "Phoenix." A third century Greek writer composed a satire, or parody, on the tale. In 1909 Gabriel d'Annunzio wrote his "Fedra." In classical Rome, the poet, Ovid, composed his own version of a letter from Phaedra to Hippolytus.

In all honesty, we have to add a word about these male victims of the false cry of rape. We said earlier, parenthetically, that, when a lady says "no" to a man, she does it in such a way as to preserve his ego. The equivalent should be true of the gentleman who turns down a female advance. Joseph, Bata, and Hippolytus, all three of them, do not behave like gentlemen. A reply on the order of: "You're the most beautiful thing I've ever seen in my life, but you know this would be wrong for us; your loveliness frightens me," would have gone a long way to avoid the dire consequences that followed in each of our tales. A simple "get lost kid, I can't handle this" might even have done the trick. But our masculine heroes climb up on their high horse (my own interpretation of the name "Hippolytus"), seize the lofty moral mountain tops for themselves, and attempt to pour guilt down the slopes onto women who, after all is said and done, are flattering these insensitive fellows more than is deserved. We have to confess that our three heroes behave in a self-centered way. In the case of Joseph, we know that he was that kind of person and remained so until late in life. He changed somewhat only in the confrontation and reunion with his family.

On the other hand, there is a factor that is seldom considered. In our society we talk a great deal about sexual harassment. In context, we refer to males who attempt to exploit female underlings. Such practices are said to be widespread in business, public life, the military services, and education. But it is not actually a one-way street. Women in controlling positions often act in a similar fashion toward men who depend on them or are expected to obey them. Just talk frankly to any door-to-door salesman, milkman, clergyman, or others who have to work with or for women. It is plain that the Joseph-Hippolytus–Bata dilemma is not unique. It is equally clear that this type of personality is not well equipped to handle the situation. A humbler or less self-righteous kind of man would no doubt do better under this kind of pressure. An ordinary man would probably be aware of mixed feelings in his own breast: temptation, fear, and doubt; along with moral and ethical considerations.

But we have to recognize a plain masculine fact of life. The male audiences who heard these stories and attended these plays in ancient times were not ready to put any of the blame for the tragedy on the protagonists. Male readers today are probably not prepared to do so either. Men love the theme so much because, in their own minds at least, all the onus can be shifted to the villainess.

The drift of the story is inevitably attractive to men. It is ferociously anti-feminine. Yet it touches a nerve of honest fear in the male breast. The wide dispersal of the theme throughout a vast geographical area over an immense stretch of time is testimony to its centrality. It resonates with the tones of vulnerability that men feel. Few of us are as pure as Joseph or as devoted as Bata or as strait-laced as Hippolytus. If it could happen to such men as these, then what of the rest of us? What would we do if confronted with their dilemma? How can we save ourselves from the clutches of wily women? Is there any mystery to the age-old, universal popularity of this drama?

Before we finish with it, we should admit that there may also be a sinister side to its popularity. For some men, the lesson of the story could be that we have to be very suspicious of all rape charges. Doubt can be cast on even the most seemingly convincing corroborative evidence. If this interpretation is in the back of some people's minds, it should be recognized and dispelled. Neither the Bible nor the other literary monuments we have cited suggest even a hint of such intention. All the ancient literature of which we know, the Bible above all, invariably perceive rape as a contemptible crime. Scriptural law and that of the other ancient cultures, as we shall discover, take the word of the woman over that of the man and do not even demand corroborative evidence. And without exception, the ancients, the Biblical people especially, regard rape as the fault solely of the man.

Chapter IV:
THE CONSEQUENCES OF AN ATROCITY

We tend to think of rape as a crime committed by or among individuals. One or more persons are perpetrators. One or more parties are injured. We hope that the criminal or criminals will be caught, tried, and severely punished. We want something to be done to assist the victim or victims mentally and physically. We want to believe that an effective system of justice will get rapists off the streets and deter others from following their example. It is clear to us that no mechanism operated by human beings will ever be perfect. However, we trust that there will be few false rape charges and that the enforcement apparatus will not make too many mistakes. It is easy for us to understand that people can become very angry about crime in general and rape in particular. But we are not happy when men and women take the law into their own hands. Private revenge and retaliation, we know, are dangerous. Mob action and lynchings make us realize how emotional an issue rape can be. The attempt to redress wrongs can often lead to the worst miscarriages of justice.

Rape therefor is not a private matter. The crime may take place between two private individuals. It may happen on private property. But it is a public concern. A woman's life has been changed forever. She has been physically attacked. Her rights as well as her person have been violated. She is psychologically and perhaps physically disabled and will remain so for a long time, perhaps for her whole life. She may be pregnant.

She has a family, and they are disrupted, too. Her parents had hopes for her which may now be disappointed. Her brothers and sisters grieve for her. They feel anger and fear. She may be married and the mother of children. The reaction of her husband may be very complex. His whole life can be influenced. He, himself, may feel violated. He may see her as defiled, disqualified. He may have to struggle with himself to continue to perform as a husband, a parent, a law-abiding citizen. The children, also, are not unscathed. An injury has been done them, not just their mother. The fact is that the fabric of the family is almost invariably damaged as the result of a rape. It is the family which is the basic building block of society. This causes the wave of distress to spread still farther. There is a circle of friends, a neighborhood, a community. Ultimately, the event becomes part of a national statistic. We have all suffered a painful hurt. Not just a woman, a whole society has been raped. To the extent that it can be understood rationally, this social hurt accounts in great part for our visceral, often violent, reaction to the crime of sexual assault.

That is exactly what the ancients felt when they proclaimed: "Such a thing is just not done in Israel." It is unacceptable conduct because it reaches out and violates concentric circles of humanity until the entire nation is wounded. The family, the tribe, the nation that feels itself violated along with one of its women wants to strike back. Nothing produces a rage greater than rape. It must be avenged. Our women have got to be protected. Only the blood of the fiend who did it can atone for it. String him up. Stake him out. Castrate him. Torture is too good for him. Public lashing is not enough. And the further the criminal, or the supposed criminal, is from us in race, color, language, religion, and nationality; the hotter the fury, the more righteous the indignation.

Inevitably, when men take justice into their own violent hands, they go too far. The society, through its leaders, creates law. It tries to establish social tranquility by rendering judgement and punishment in a calm, measured manner. People accept this idea gladly. It takes the burden of doing vengeance off the shoulders of individuals. It prevents the excesses that follow do-it-yourself justice. Law does all those things when it works. Then we speak of law and order. We establish due process and trial by jury. The system is impersonal and even-handed with equal justice for all. We hope. The trouble comes when the system loses its balance. In crime-plagued, drug-ridden America, it often seems that the establishment has gone wrong. The police are handcuffed instead of the criminals. The law-abiding people, but not the wrongdoers, spend their time behind locked and even barred doors and windows. The danger for our community today is the sense of frustration that the people have with the instruments of law enforcement. The criminals, many people often feel, have all the rights; the victims none. The murdered man never appears at the trial. The rape victim is violated once again on the witness stand.

When many people begin to feel that way, democracy is in danger. If the time ever comes when the nation has to choose between law and order, the majority may well desire the latter. To preserve our freedoms, we have to make law work. We have to restore the balance between reasonable due process and the need to punish the guilty. If the law is ever pushed aside, we go back to the caves, the jungle, the blood feud. It has taken humanity a long time to get where we are now, just how long we will see in a moment. The social progress we have made is too valuable a thing to lose. Law and liberty are at stake, and it will pay us to heed the moral lesson that comes down to us from antiquity.

In their time, the last three chapters of the book of Judges were edited and published as propaganda pieces of the first order. With the subtlety of a pile driver, they slam home the message that Israel needs a king, the nation must be consolidated, tribal disorganization can no longer be tolerated. The need for a union headed by a king is the central message of the final editor of the book of Judges. To make his point, this editor drew upon the record of a sexual assault as savage as anything we can imagine.

The very name of the book is probably a mistranslation. The Hebrew word 'shofteem" should be understood to mean "rescuers" or possibly "protectors," in the context of this Biblical book. Very likely, the leaders who are described here also served as judges, and that may account for the fact that the Hebrew word takes on the meaning of judge (and retains it in modern Hebrew until this day). When we first meet Deborah in chapter four (Ju.4.5) she is acting as a judge in the legalistic sense of the term. But she is also described as a prophetess, and her main role in the Biblical account is to serve as a military leader and an inspiration against the Canaanite oppressors. All of the rescuers, in the first eighteen chapters of Judges, serve to save Israel from foreign enemies. Only the last three chapters deal with an internal problem. But that problem has such severe effects that it becomes the celebrated cause to make a case for the crowning of a king over Israel. Although no king was anointed for another hundred years or so, the events in the book of Judges, this final bloody event in particular, no doubt remained fresh in the popular memory.

We should point out that there was also a body of anti-royalist sentiment that remained active in ancient Israel until the last minute. Most of the writers whose work remains as the bulk of the material in the book of Judges were, in fact, theocrats and anti-royalists. The drift of most of the episodes in the book follows a set pattern, probably indicating one writer or one committee of writers who all saw eye to eye on the king issue. In most of the stories, the people of Israel sin by forgetting God and worshipping idols. The Lord sends an enemy to punish Israel. When they are hard pressed by the foe, the people get religion, pray to Yahveh, and He sends a rescuer who saves them through war against the enemy. But the people soon slide back into their old ways, and the entire process has to be repeated. None of the rescuers will consent to become king. Some specifically refuse the crown. Gideon is the parade example of the protector who chooses to remain a private citizen when the battle is over, even though the populace offers him a hereditary throne. He replies (Ju.8.23): "Neither I nor my descendants will rule you. Yahveh will rule you."

The concept behind this counter current was the conviction that Israel already had a king, God. Israel was not like the other nations. They might be ruled by human kings. The Ruler of Israel was the King of kings. The most eloquent expression of anti-king feelings, maybe the strongest anti-government statement in all human literature, is found in chapter eight of First Samuel (1Sam.8.11-18). Deuteronomic laws governing the behavior of the king of Israel also sound as if they were written to correct abuses that had already occurred. In fact, they appear to refer rather directly to Solomon's conduct of office. (Deut.17.14-20). But quite clearly, between the two schools of thought: 1) We are not like the other nations, God is our King, and we do not need human government and 2) We should be like the other nations, appoint a king for us; the royalists ultimately won the day. The choice they made affected them not only in ancient times, but it also determined the shape of Jewish (and ultimately of Christian) theology.(7)

The series of events that played such a central part in the making of this fateful decision is reported in the last three chapters of Judges. It proceeds from the report of a vicious gang rape to a call for vengeance to outright civil war to the near extermination of an entire tribe. We shall review the account now.

Judges nineteen reports that at an undetermined time before there was a king in Israel, a Levite man lived as a resident stranger in the outskirts of the hill country of Ephraim. He is unnamed. In fact, all the characters involved in this account are nameless. We are told that he was a Levite. But he does not appear to have performed any of the ritualistic functions we might associate with members of that tribe. It seems that we are dealing with a very early time, before the Levites were assigned the exclusive rights to religious leadership. For other reasons that we will take up later, it is likely that this narrative, though placed at the end of the book of Judges, is one of the earliest, if not the earliest, of the events related in that book. Be that as it may, this man has a wife of low social standing, a concubine who leaves him. The reason for her leaving is not entirely clear. Our Hebrew text indicates that she went astray sexually, perhaps even practiced prostitution. The exact terminology is not really clear. But the ancient Greek and Latin translators were working from a text with a different Hebrew reading. Those writers rendered the text to the effect that she became angry with him. At any rate, she goes back home to her father in Bethlehem, Judah.

After four months, the husband travels south to Bethlehem to try and persuade her to return to Ephraim. He takes along a servant and a pair of donkeys. The couple reunites, and she brings him in to her father's house for a visit. The father-in-law is glad to see him. He invites the Levite and his wife to enjoy his hospitality. They stay with him for several days; well provided with food, drink, and lodging. One morning when they rise early, the Levite decides that this is the day for them to leave. But the woman's father urges him to have a hearty meal first. Then he and his wife and servant can go. The two men sit down to a great repast, and a good deal of time goes by. So when the man insists that his son-in-law spend one more night with him, the latter consents. The next day the Levite is again importuned to have a good meal before leaving. Once more, time passes; and the woman's father urges his guest to stay just one more day. But, though the day has begun to wear on, the Levite makes a final, as it turns out, fateful decision to be off.

About four miles north of Bethlehem they reach Jebus, the Canaanite city that will be the future site of Jerusalem. The daylight is fast disappearing, and the servant suggests that they spend the night within the safety of the city walls. But the master responds: "We shall not turn aside into an alien city that is not of the Israelites. We shall go on to Gibeah (Ju.19.12)." There is to be great irony in the sentiment which the Levite expresses here. He is afraid for their safety if they come into a Canaanite city as strangers. He desires to go on to Gibeah, an Israelite and Benjaminite settlement, less than three miles further on to the north. He is saying implicitly that they can expect security and hospitality among their own. His judgement about their ability to cover ground is also not very good. He states that they may even be able to make Ramah, a town another three miles or so beyond Gibeah.

But the sun sets on them near Gibeah, the Benjaminite city. They enter the town and sit down in the main square. But no one invites them in or offers them lodging. Finally an old man comes in for the night from his work in the fields. He is from the hills of Ephraim, where the Levite resides. And this man is a resident stranger among the Benjaminites of Gibeah. The old man notices the visitor. He asks the Levite where he comes from and where he is going. When he hears the answer, especially impressed perhaps by the fact that the Levite is from his own native area, and learns that no one has extended hospitality, he invites the troop of travelers to spend the night with him.(8) He will see to all their needs and even provide feed for the animals. He is most insistent that they not camp out in the open square.

He brings all of them into his house. He feeds the donkeys. He washes the feet of his guests and provides them with food and drink. But while they are all enjoying themselves, an ugly crowd is gathering outside the door of the house. The men of the city, characterized in the text as lawless persons,(9) demand that the old man send out his guest to them so that they may "know" him. There is virtually no doubt that sexual, carnal knowledge is intended here. The host comes out into the street and pleads with the lawless ones. He is certainly taking a terrible risk in order to defend his guests. Though an outsider himself, he calls the people "my bothers." He begs them not to do evil to a guest under his protection and not to commit this vile act.

They remain insistent. Now he offers them his own virgin daughter and the guest's concubine to ravish as they will, if they will only refrain from carrying out their disgusting intent. But the men refuse to listen to him. At this point, the Levite seems to decide to work things out his own way. To protect himself, and perhaps to save the tender virgin, he seizes his concubine (she is no longer called his wife) and turns her over to the men in the street. They violate her and assault her throughout the night and release her only at dawn. She staggers to the old man's house and falls on the doorstep. Her master emerges in the morning, ready to continue on his journey. He finds "the woman, his concubine," fallen at the entrance of the house with her hands on the threshold. He orders her to rise so that they can be off, but there is no answer. The Biblical writer does not tell us explicitly; but we know, of course, that she is dead. He loads the body on one of the donkeys and carries it back home with him.

Students and readers of the Bible will, inevitably, draw comparisons between this account and that in the nineteenth chapter of the book of Genesis. We can take a look at that passage now, before going on with a discussion of the consequences of the atrocity at Gibeah. In Genesis, Lot, the nephew of Abraham, has moved to Sodom. It is a city, along with Gomorrah, that has displeased God. We are told that there is an outcry from these two cities and that their sin is weighty. But we are given no specifics. God sends two of His messengers (sometimes called “men” in this narrative) to see if things are really so bad. The problem for both translators and theologians is that the Hebrew word ‘malakh’ means both messenger and angel, as does the Greek word ‘angelos’, from which our word “angel” comes. Be that as it may, the two of them arrive in Sodom in the evening. Lot is sitting at the gate of the city, the public meeting place. He sees them and invites them, in exquisitely polite terms, to spend the night with him. They put him off, saying that they will lodge in the main square (Hebrew ‘r’khov’, the exact same word as in Judges). After a while, they give in to his urging and come to his house. He makes a meal for them and bakes unleavened bread. Just as they are ready to go to bed, the entire male population surrounds the house. The men of Sodom shout for the two men to be brought out “so that we may know them.” Lot comes out in the street, locking the door behind him. He pleads: “My brothers, do not do evil (Gen.19.7).” He offers his two daughters, whom no man has known. They may do as they like with them. But the Sodomites must not touch the men who have come under Lot’s protection. The people mock Lot as the outsider who has now come to sit in judgement on them. They press Lot hard and approach to break open the door. But now the two visitors resolve the conflict. They pull Lot away from the mob, lock the door, and strike all the men of Sodom with blindness. The attackers give up trying to find the door. The messengers-angels then proceed to rescue Lot and his family before the destruction of the city.

The differences between the two accounts are plain. In Judges, we are dealing with the world as we know it. The events described could be on the front pages of our papers tomorrow morning. In Genesis, we are in the midst of a heavily theologized tale. But the similarities are inescapable. The lawless ones at Gibeah and the men of Sodom are more interested in homosexual rape than anything else. They will accept heterosexual assault only as a poor second choice (although the Sodomites never get the chance). Both narratives are charged with a message about hospitality. The Gibeah violence is preceded by the story of the Levite's protracted stay with his father-in-law in Bethlehem. The men-messengers-angels come to Sodom directly from the splendid reception they have just received in Abraham's tents. In both cases, it is resident strangers who step forward to extend a welcome. Implicitly, the reader or listener in Biblical times would know from the start that the town where no native makes the offer of hospitality must be a very bad place. He or she would not be surprised that terrible, violent things might happen next. It may be hard for us to take, but an additional similarity in values is common to the two accounts. It is to the host's honor that he can offer up his virgin daughters in order to protect the guest for whom he has taken responsibility. There is no stigma attached even when the Levite throws his own wife to the wolves. (One does not have to wonder too much as to why she left him in the first place.)

However, there is one vast difference that we cannot ignore. Sodom is destroyed by God's will because of its crimes. Gibeah, as we shall see, is destroyed under quite other circumstances. The message of the Sodom and Gomorrah story is that God acts justly and sends just punishment for the wicked. Trust in God and all will be well. The message of the Gibeah report is that, without a king, men will act vengefully. Tribal men make feuds. If you want justice, you need a king.

We might speculate about the relationship between the two passages. There are endless possibilities. The only one we cannot accept is that the resemblance is accidental, simple coincidence. For our purposes, let us dwell on just two of the possible interpretations. 1) The Sodom tale was an old tradition, known at the time of the Gibeah incident in more or less the form in which we have it. When it came time to write up the Gibeah account, conscious effort was employed to stress the similarity of circumstances; as if to say: Look at these lawless people of Gibeah. They act like the men of Sodom. They deserve the same punishment, total destruction. Or 2) The telling of the Sodom story was recast after the Gibeah incident so as to stress the common factors. This would serve to criticize the Israelites for the way in which the aftermath of Gibeah was handled. The near complete destruction of the tribe of Benjamin (which we will cover next) was an unjust, ill-considered act. But it should not be exploited as reason to demand a king. This was a way of proclaiming: If you had waited with trust in God, He would have punished the guilty city in his own way, just as He did Sodom. God is all you need. He is your true king. Wait patiently, and He will always give you justice.

The second formulation rings a little truer than the first from a critical point of view. But, for our purposes, it is not decisive. We are most interested in the value system of the men who wrote these stories. The important thing is the horror they felt toward rape. The fact is that both the royalists and theocrats could agree on their abhorrence of sexual violence. When they argued their mutually antagonistic causes, both sides honored the same set of values as to hospitality and justice. They were equally enraged over sexual assault. Both sides recognized the social character of the crime. They were agreed that rape deserved retribution. Rape, therefor, could be a wand for political conjuring. To affect the masses of humanity, however, a cause must be presented effectively. The Levite finds a striking, if not quite unique, manner in which to state his case.

The Levite brings the outraged body of his wife-concubine back home. He takes his knife and cuts the corpse into twelve parts. These he sends throughout all the tribes of Israel.(10) He draws upon an old tradition, as we know, in spreading the word in this manner. While his approach is not wholly new, we are aware of no other incidence when human remains were employed in such a direct way. The effects are immediate. The last verse of chapter nineteen (Ju.19.30) tells us: "Such a thing has never been seen since the people of Israel came up out of Egypt! Take notice of it! Take counsel! Speak out!"

We will not discuss in detail all the events described in the last two chapters of the book of Judges. The entire nation gathers, all the men of an age for military service. The Levite reports the terrible deed that has been done. His story is fairly accurate. He indicates, however, that the entire male population surrounded the house. It will be recalled that in the previous chapter there was just a band of lawless fellows at the door. The Levite makes it sound exactly like Sodom. He tells the people that his own life was in danger, and that the Gibeans wanted to rape his concubine. He does not refer to the threat of sexual assault to his own person. He omits entirely the fact that it was he who cast the woman out into the night to meet her fate.

Even in those days, he might have realized that his act demonstrated a certain lack of gallantry.

The entire nation now organizes for war. When the Benjaminites realize what is happening, that the intent is to destroy a city in their territory, they make a costly decision. The entire tribe takes the side of Gibeah. Here, after all, there is a chance to control events. If the Benjaminites could proclaim that they will see justice done, they might be able to forestall the impending disaster. But the tribal system leaves the leaders of Benjamin no leeway. The military strength of the tribe is the only real law they can rely on. The members of the tribe, and the communities in every tribe, are solidly bonded together in a covenant relationship. This binds Israelites together against outsiders, that is its strength. But it also binds tribal members together, even against their own people from other tribes. It is this that brings about the catastrophe. There is no central authority, no king, who can now step in and stop the massacre by enforcing the law justly and effectively. The very structure of the culture compels every Benjaminite to come to Gibeah's aid.

Enormous numbers of men are mustered on each side. A three day battle follows in which the Benjaminites defend themselves with great success. Israelite casualties are very heavy. But then the tribes reorganize their order of battle. They appear to engage in frontal attack as before and to flee when they are under pressure. But they lead the Benjaminites, who think that victory is at hand again, into a series of prepared ambushes. Gibeah falls and is destroyed.(11) But now, as happens often in the heat of battle, the original cause of the war is forgotten. No one declares that now that the sinful community has been punished, we can all go home. Instead, the tribes turn their attack against all the helpless people of Benjamin; men, women, and children. That tribe is all but exterminated.

The men of the other tribes even take an irreversible oath that they will never give any of their daughters as wives to the few Benjaminite survivors.

When tempers cool, the people realize what they have done and seek ways to reverse it. They cannot break the oath they made to the Lord. But how else can they save the tribe of Benjamin, their brothers, from extinction. Scripture presents two different ways in which they solved the problem. It is not unlikely that there is some historical truth in each of them. The first of these traditions relates that the leaders review the muster and realize that the men of Jabesh Gilead did not participate in the battle. Without any attempt at negotiation, they send an army against the city, destroy it, kill all the males and married women, and bring back four hundred virgins as brides for Benjamin. While the leaders' approach to the problem may seem a bit extreme, one must remember that there is probably a feeling among them that the men of Jabesh Gilead are shirkers who deserve no better.

The other tradition is lawless, but not so violent. At the festival when the unmarried girls come out to dance in the vineyards, the Benjaminites are instructed to seize the virgins of Shiloh and carry them off as wives. If the men of Shiloh object, the leaders will dissuade them from action. If they protest that they swore never to give wives to Benjamin, the leaders will answer that no women were given voluntarily, therefor the oath was not violated. Thus, in one or both of these fashions, the tribe of Benjamin is restored. At any rate, we know from scripture that by the time of Saul, the Benjaminite, it is once again a great and powerful tribe. Moreover, it is the tribe which merits the honor of providing Israel's first king. In its way, the anointing of Saul rounds out the message of the book of Judges. The last verse of the book (Ju.21.25) hammers home the concept, as if we had not already gotten the message. "At that time there was no king in Israel. Anyone could do whatever he pleased."

It would certainly be wrong, and unfair to our subject, to go on at this point without at least some reference to the act of carrying off the girls of Shiloh. After all, the original meaning of the antecedents of the very word "rape" in Old English was "to seize and take away by force." Without so much as the slightest thought about the pain and tears which the removal of the maidens of Shiloh must have caused to the girls themselves, as well as to their families, scripture not only stomachs but seems actually to approve of the act. It seems to us like the last in a chain of mounting injustices that began with the atrocity at Gibeah. Even from the grossest, most chauvinistic masculine standpoint, the fathers of the Shiloh girls are deprived of any compensation for the loss of a valuable asset, their marriageable daughters, for whom they should have been entitled to a bride price. The writers and editor of Judges seem unconcerned about this. They probably breathe a sigh of relief that the serious dilemma of the perishing tribe of Benjamin can be solved in such a relatively straightforward manner.

Readers inevitably will think of the rape of the Sabine women by the early Romans. The tale is generally dismissed as myth. And the concept of "myth" in such cases means "made up out of the whole cloth." It should be left to specialists in the field, however, to say whether or not we are dealing in this case with another of those elements common to the culture of the ancient eastern Mediterranean.

To speculate on a possible relationship between the Levite in our account and the role of Levi, along with his brother Simeon, in the case of the rape of Dinah, would be fruitless. What is common between the events, however, is very real. That shared factor is, quite simply, overreaction.

After the destruction of the people of Shechem, Jacob is ashamed and fearful. He moves out of the district. After the near extermination of the Benjaminites, the leaders are overwhelmed at what they have done. They resort to drastic measures to correct the situation. In both cases, we are dealing with men who are infuriated, nay maddened, when they learn of a particular rape. In the one instance, it is because the rape is too close to home; in the other, because of the intensity of the violence and the propagandizing skill of the Levite. There are specific individuals that are guilty in both cases. At Shechem, there is one definite perpetrator. At Gibeah, at least until the Levite tells the story, there is a large, but limited, band of lawless men. In both situations, however, the offended men hold the entire community to blame. All of Shechem, all of Benjamin are wiped out in a fury of savagery. We may refer to the Hebrew or Semitic or Eastern Mediterranean concept of community responsibility. But that cannot account fully for the events in the reports we have analyzed.

We are dealing with profound psychological matters about which men are sensitive. An author who is a simple student of the Bible and its languages is no doubt foolish to rush into the precincts of the specialist in the psychological sciences. But sometimes the wren finds prey where eagles dare not perch. This writer is far from his area of expertise, but perhaps not so far from right, in suggesting the workings of a psychological process. We love the movie where the good guy takes the first punch on his own jaw and then beats up the villain. The best boxing match is where one of the fighters takes a licking and then gets up off the mat at the nine count to down the other fellow. Many people agreeably follow the film plot where an act of violence, often one or more rapes, serves to justify an hour or two of heroic brutality in revenge. In contrast to our

Bible passages, however, no one ever seems to show remorse for all the overblown outrages that take place. In the celluloid world, even the cops often wink at these vengeful excesses. In this last type of movie, as in the two passages of scripture to which we refer, the fury of the response goes far beyond the level of any reasonable punishment for the miscreants. That high level of violence must be in the human heart all the time, then. The initial rape, or other violent act, releases all that pent-up savagery. Is it too much for us to guess that there are men who welcome the news that rapes and outrages have taken place so that they can legitimately, if not legally, resort to their own rampage of violence. This writer has heard male friends confess or admit to fantasies to the effect that their mothers or sisters or wives or daughters were assaulted, as justification for subsequent imaginary unbridled acts of brutal retaliation on their own part. Other men, we must say, come back at us with overheated vehemence at the very suggestion that such thoughts might exist in the male breast. The thermal level of their reaction often makes one feel that their protest might just be a little overdone. Be all that as it may. The writer apologizes for dabbling in the realms of psyche. The fact that emerges from all our speculation is that there are powerful wellsprings of violence buried not so deep in humanity. More than three thousand years since our Bible stories were composed, nothing much has changed.

What did develop was a system of laws that attempted to deal with criminality on a controlled plane. By the seventh century B.C., Deuteronomic law proclaimed: "If you should hear that, in one of the cities which the Lord your God gives you, lawless men have gone forth and corrupted the inhabitants, urging them to worship unknown other gods; then you shall 'inquire' 'searchingly' and 'thoroughly' [our emphasis]. Then, if the accusation is true, strike down the inhabitants of that city at the edge of the sword. Wipe it out, along with everything in it....Totally burn all its booty to the Lord....It shall never be rebuilt. (Deut.13.13ff.)" Such a law not only seems excessive to us now, it was, in time, made unenforceable by the classic rabbis. They insisted that every single member of the offending community must have a formal warning. In the context of rabbinic law, that means that each individual has to be told the nature of his infraction by two qualified warners (who cannot later be witnesses against him). The warners must also impart precise information as to the possible punishment the wrongdoer might incur.(12) Obviously, if measures in the spirit of the original Biblical law had been taken against Gibeah to start with, the greater calamity would probably have been avoided.

But that is not yet the message of the book of Judges. Its writers and editor are at odds with one another over the issue of whether or not Israel needs a king. The final, controlling editor insists that a strong central leader is required to keep things in order. Once there is a king, runs the argument, such injustices will not happen. But the next episode we consider happens at a time when there is a king in Israel, possibly the greatest king that Israel ever had, and things still go wrong. He has trouble running the nation because he cannot govern his own family and will not punish his own son for incestuous rape.

Chapter V:
ANOTHER TAMAR, AND QUITE A LADY

All the thunder and lightning of the book of Judges did not have the desired political effect immediately. Israel limped on through the twelfth and much of the eleventh centuries B.C. as a loosely structured federation of tribes. The royalists and the theocrats argued away without arriving at any decisive conclusion. Each threat from any of the Canaanite peoples or from the nations in Trans-Jordan was dealt with on a piecemeal basis. Leaders rose to meet each emergency, muster the people, fight off the menace, and then retire to private life. With the Lord's help, Israel muddled its way from crisis to crisis.

But the coming of the sea peoples, the ones the Bible calls the Philistines, changed everything. In the Greek Islands there were severe demographic pressures. New elements, non-Semitic populations, invaded Greece and the Islands. Geological catastrophe struck in the form of the enormous eruption of the volcano at Thera (Santorini). The tidal wave from the eruption inundated Minoan civilization. All these factors drove masses from the Islands to seek new homes on the shores of the eastern Mediterranean. They invaded every soft point they could find, from Asia Minor to Egypt. Among the places where they managed to establish beachheads was the land to which they were to give their name, Palestine. They settled five cities on and near the seacoast. But by the eleventh century B.C., they were attacking the hill country, the very territory in which the Israelites were struggling to consolidate their own conquest.

The Philistine challenge tipped the balance in the controversy over the need for a king in Israel. Under protest, Samuel anointed Saul as the first king. But Saul turned out to be inadequate as a leader. The Philistines crushed him in battle and threatened to swallow up Israel. Saul's talents and character were not equal to the task. And Saul came from the minor tribe of Benjamin. The Judean, David, who followed him possessed everything that Saul lacked. David came from the largest and most powerful of the tribes. He was a man of prodigious versatility. Scripture remembers David as an accomplished musician and poet, a literary and religious genius, a military and political leader of the highest quality. Above all, David's political and public relations decisions were flawless. He was the consummate politician.

David conquered Jerusalem and made it the capital of Israel. The location of the city was all-important because it lay outside the territory of any of the tribes. David defeated the Philistines and subjugated them to such a degree that they never again posed any problem for the Israelites. He completely dominated the remnants of Canaanite civilization and subdued all of Israel's enemies on the eastern side of the Jordan river, Moab and Ammon and Edom. He took Elat and controlled all the available trade routes that connected the various parts of the ancient Middle East. No one could deliver a camel load of goods over any distance without paying tribute to David and Israel. He won the most humiliating trade concessions from Syria and held Egypt at bay throughout his reign. In brief, David conquered vast territories and built a mighty empire. He brought security to his people after they had known nothing but centuries of terror before their enemies. He brought unheard of wealth to a nation that had been living at the subsistence level.

David was a great public figure. Few have been his equal in political and cultural accomplishments. He ran an empire with relative ease. But his personal life was a dreadful failure. His early marriages were all unsatisfactory. His later marriages seem to have been politically motivated. To achieve his one happy marriage, he became a murderer and adulterer. But he was especially weak in dealing with his children, and his irresolute performance as a parent nearly cost him his throne.

The Bible's book of Second Samuel could have more accurately been called the book of David. King David is its central figure from beginning to end. Samuel, on the other hand, is dead before the book's history begins. It relates how David inherited Saul's throne and slowly crushed opposition on the part of pretenders who rose from Saul's family. David reigned for years in Hebron in Judah before the conquest of Jerusalem, somewhere around 1000 B.C. In Hebron he made several marriages. With Ahinoam of Jezreel, he had his first son, Amnon. After the birth of another son, Chileab, by Abigail the widow of Nabal of Carmel, he had children with a princess from Geshur in the Golan heights, Maacah. She bore him a son, Absalom, and later a daughter, Tamar.

Whether or not this Tamar is named after David's ancient forebear, the Tamar who progressed from a role as Judah's daughter-in-law to wife-consort, is immaterial. Her mother is a princess, her grandfather and father, kings. She has the regal bearing and a character of boundless power, she is a renowned beauty, and her half-brother Amnon is in love with her. His character is as weak as hers is strong. His manner is not that of the eldest prince and presumed heir to the throne. It is the carriage of a spoiled infant.

Chapter thirteen of Second Samuel reports a story of love, rape, hate, and vengeance. The tale is really set in the midst of the account of Absalom's political aspirations and his ultimate revolt against his doting father. So once again rape and politics mix in the Biblical mind. Once more, the Bible recounts the record of a rape because we must understand it in order to grasp the shape of greater, public events. We are told that Amnon is so painfully in love that his health deteriorates. His sickness is compounded by the fact that Tamar is a virgin princess. She is no doubt well guarded, and Amnon feels that there is absolutely nothing he can do to her. The prince pines away helplessly until he gets a word of advice from a friendly cousin, Jonadab, the son of one of David's brothers, Shimeah. Jonadab is a clever fellow. Perhaps he sees his main chance someday to become the chief advisor to the future king. He notices how weak Amnon looks every morning and asks him why. Amnon confesses his love for Tamar. Interestingly enough, Tamar here is identified not as the daughter of the king, but as the "sister of Absalom, my brother (2Sam.13.4)." Amnon already feels this brother's hot breath on the back of his neck. When he fears that he cannot do anything to Tamar, Absalom's growing following and powerful influence are probably uppermost in Amnon's mind. Jonadab has an instant plan. He sees that the prince does not look too well to begin with. The friend suggests that Amnon get in bed and play sick. This will bring a visit from the king. And when the royal father asks what can be done to help, Jonadab puts the reply into the crown prince's mouth. Amnon is to tell David (2Sam.13.5): "Please let my sister, Tamar, come to feed me. She can make the food while I watch, and then I will eat it out of her hand." The king, indeed, does come to pay a sick call. Amnon, embroidering a little on the script, follows his cousin's counsel. The king takes in every word, and is taken in. David, the iron-willed monarch with his subjects, is always ready to be manipulated by his spoiled children. He falls for the ruse.

David sends a message to Tamar's house, requesting that she go to her sick brother and make food for him. She complies. While he watches from his bed, she prepares dough and kneads it. She flattens it out and makes pancakes. It is possible from the language that these cakes were made in the shape of hearts and conveyed some symbolic point, at least in Amnon's mind.(13) The princess is ready to come to Amnon with the pan in her hand to serve him personally, but he still refuses to eat. He commands that all the people leave the house so that he can be alone with Tamar when she feeds him. They comply, and Amnon asks Tamar to come into his room so that he can eat out of her hand. She brings the food into his bedchamber. When she approaches to feed him, Amnon grabs her and tells her to get into bed with him. If we had any doubts as to Amnon's immaturity and narcissism, they are dispelled when we see the crudity of his approach to Tamar. The young woman, on the other hand, keeps her head throughout her disagreeable experience. She answers his demand with (2Sam.13.12): "Don't, my brother. Don't rape me, because this is something that is just not done in Israel. Do not commit this disgraceful act."

This is the first of Tamar's attempts to make her brother think about what he is doing. She lets him know immediately that she will not give in and does not reciprocate his sentiments. Her appeal to him is based on the plain fact that, if he rapes her, it will not be a simple, private crime. The act will be made public immediately, and the consequences will be serious. In plain language she would have informed him that she would tell, and David and/or Absalom would kill him. But she is not talking to a reasonable, mature man. Her brother, Amnon, is a spoiled brat, the heir apparent, who feels that he is above the law. He persists.

Next Tamar tries to get him to see her as a person, not just an object for his pleasure. "Where will I take my shame (v.13)?"she asks him. And again she tries to make him consider the repercussions for himself. She tells him that he will become a pariah in Israel. But these importunings are also useless.

As a last, desperate attempt to forestall the outrage, Tamar makes a statement that, under ordinary conditions, might have appealed to Amnon (v.13b). "Now speak to the king. He will not deny me to you." There is just a chance that Amnon will listen. After all, the king has probably never refused his son anything. We have to doubt, however, that David would have been ready to swallow the idea of incest in the royal family. Amnon does not believe it either. Besides, he is used to getting what he wants when he wants it. He attacks Tamar, and she puts up a fight. But he is too strong for her. He rapes her.

And now he hates her. Scripture informs us that the hatred he feels for her right after the act is greater than the love he had for her beforehand. He orders her out, but she does not want to leave. To be thrown out now, she senses, will prevent any chance she may have to make things right in her subsequent life. She tells him that dismissing her is a worse wrong than the one he has already committed. But again Amnon will not listen. He calls his servant to put her out of the house.

But this is quite a woman. She has already been more than Amnon bargained for. What did he expect? That when he asked her to bed she would meekly comply? That after he raped her she would fall in love with him? (Some men seem to have that delusion.) Did he expect her to yield because no one ever denied him anything? Tamar has conducted herself with strength throughout her ordeal. The terse way in which the Bible relates the story leaves the details to our imagination. We can only imagine the way she struggles. We can picture the expressionless face she shows him while he is having her; her limp, motionless, unresponsive, insulting body. The contempt she communicates to him is plain to us. What else could have earned this sudden reversal of love into hate?

Trying to talk one's way out of a rape is a questionable tactic. We cannot know much about its effectiveness. If there are many women who have succeeded in avoiding violation in this manner, we know little or nothing of them. It is not something that a woman would be eager to discuss later. Tamar tells Amnon that the act he contemplates is something just not done. It will harm her as a person. It is abominable; doubly so since it is incest as well as sexual assault. She warns him that he will be ostracized. She tickles him with the thought that their father, the King, has the power to legitimize a marriage between them.

All of this is well and good. But we could have predicted that it would have no effect on the Prince. Tamar is speaking on a level to which Amnon is simply not attuned. Her arguments are rational. Amnon is in an emotional frenzy. The rapist seldom thinks through the act he is going to commit. It is unlikely that his motivations, calling them reasons would be going too far, can be explained in rational terms. The probability is that no two rapists are exactly alike. The chances of dissuading one of them are slim, therefor. Is he exerting power? Does he hate all women? Is this a blow at society, parental authority, an overbearing mother? Is he an out and out lunatic or a pathological personality? Has he selected his victim, as Amnon did, or is she a random target? Is he striking at the victim's family, as Amnon may have, consciously or otherwise, struck at Absalom and the King? Or -- we might add a thousand such questions, but where would that leave us?

Whether or not to talk, scream, fight, or resist at all is something a woman has to decide for herself. No man is in a position to give generalized advice on such a situational problem. The victim must judge how violent this particular man may become. If he has a lethal weapon, only the woman in the actual situation can make up her mind whether she wants to risk injury or death. But if one does determine to talk, then an attempt has to be made to speak to 'his' needs and not to plead, as Tamar does, on the basis of hers. Questions may be better than declarative statements. "Why are you doing this?" "Have you ever committed rape before?" These could be useful. If the woman asks: "What would your mother think of you now?" she could be taking her life in her hands. And a put-down: "Is this the only way you can get it?" or "Is this the only way you can get off?" could be fatal. Any man, including this writer, should feel ridiculous trying to give women guidance on the subject. Normal men know as little about rapists as women do. A man's training and instinct are to fight, not talk, his way out of any confrontation. But faced with overwhelming force, a man, too, must contemplate the alternatives of running, talking, screaming, or yielding. Who are we to give counsel?

This is as good or bad a place to add one additional note. Rape of males by males is certainly not as common as the victimizing of women, but it is not rare. Physically, homosexual rape is possibly less harmful. Pregnancy is not a factor. But psychologically, the violation of a man is probably as devastating, or more so, than that of a woman. Although there is a good deal of law and lore hostile to homosexuality, ancient near eastern literature, including scripture, contains practically nothing on the subject of sexual assault on males. The physical strength of the victim makes little difference. The rapist or the gang of rapists are basically cowards to begin with. He or they will surely pick a victim whom they know they can subdue. Or they will arm themselves so as to make resistance unlikely and ineffective. When a man is cast in the role of victim, his means of resistance or escape, and his chances of talking his way out, are probably quite the same as those of a woman.

Scripture gives us an excellent picture of a woman trying to talk her way out of being raped. Tamar does the best she can, and the Bible also implies that she fought as hard as she could physically. But does she scream? Later, when we discuss the Biblical laws about rape, the question of screaming for help will arise. So how about Tamar? The Bible gives no indication of an answer. We have no right to argue from silence one way or the other. But we can judge that she would know how futile it would be to cry out. The only people near by are the crafty friend, Jonadab, the servant, and an undetermined number of Amnon's retinue. None of them will come to Tamar's help. All of them probably know from the beginning about the trap that is going to be sprung. Every one of them is likely to be thinking about how to stay in the good graces of the future ruler of the country. By keeping quiet now they have everything to gain and nothing to lose. Tamar is going to be ruined. Amnon may be hurt or killed. But these children of the men whom David has made newly rich will think of no one but themselves. Tamar knows all of this. But there may be another consideration in her mind. Despite her implied threat beforehand to tell all, she may now be determined to keep the crime a secret in order to preserve whatever she can of her life. When she asks Amnon not to send her away, she is ready to commit herself to silence, for both their sakes. She is willing to have it this way for a very simple reason. In order to destroy him, she would have to destroy herself. When he refuses this alternative, she no longer has any choice. She must be the one to make the deed public.

When the servant ejects Tamar from the house and locks the door on her, she is wearing the garment of the royal children, the striped coat. For this garb, scripture uses the same Hebrew expression as it does in referring to Joseph's striped coat, the famous coat of many colors given him by a doting father. The Bible says that the virgin daughters of the king were allowed to wear this coat. Tamar, still a pretty cool customer after all her tribulation, puts ashes on her head and tears the coat and walks along shrieking. She has taken upon herself all the formal signs of grief for the world to see. She heads toward the house of Absalom, and when he sees her he seems to know immediately what has happened.

Absalom has his own fish to fry. He is plotting to put himself in a position to inherit or usurp the throne. He would like to eliminate Amnon from the scene. But he is not yet ready to make his move, and any overt action against the heir apparent at this time does not suit his plans. Even more, the disgrace brought on his sister by Amnon gives Absalom the kind of opportunity any politician loves. He is in a win-win situation. If punishment is to be meted out to Amnon, or vengeance exacted, Absalom is not the one whom the people will expect to take the primary responsibility. The king is the ruler of Israel. David is the father of Tamar. The ball is in King David's court. David must walk a fine line. If he overreacts, the public is likely to remember the lessons of Shechem and Gibeah. People will say that the king should not be above the law. If David, on the other hand, fails to take any measures against Amnon, then Absalom can throw up his hands as if to ask everyone whether they cannot understand that this once great man now gone weak must be replaced. Absalom is licking his chops.

But he must silence Tamar, at least for a time. She has come to him and not to the king. She senses that David will not do anything to his pampered favorite. Now the brother, because of his own political considerations, has to put her off. Absalom tells her (2Sam.13.20): "If Amnon (the text has 'Aminon,' an alternative form of the name) has been with you, keep quiet. He is your brother. Pay no attention to the matter." Tamar accepts this judgement. Perhaps she gives in to despair, thinking that if Absalom will not help there is nowhere else to turn. Or maybe she understands what is at stake and knows or suspects how complicated the situation is for her full brother, in light of his intentions and ambitions. At any rate, she settles down in Absalom's house as a ruined woman. The king hears about what has happened and is enraged. Absalom stops talking to Amnon because of the rape. Now he can be an enemy of the heir to the throne, not for political reasons, but on a personal basis. But neither the king nor Absalom does a thing. In this atmosphere of hate and rage, of scheming and conspiracy, two years elapse.

To us business-like westerners, two years may seem a long time to wait for justice. But Absalom is not in any hurry. Firstly, the longer vengeance simmers, the more tasty the dish. A modern Arab proverb is said to run to the effect that a man must apologize to the members of his family if he takes vengeance on the enemy after only twenty years. Impatience ruins the flavor of the act. The longer one waits, the more the enemy suffers, knowing that the blow will come, but not knowing when or where or how. Amnon knows beyond the shadow of a doubt because Absalom is not speaking to him all this time. But Amnon, probably still as immature as ever, may not understand Absalom's second reason for delaying action. Politically speaking, every day that goes by puts added stress on the fact that David has not taken care of the matter. As king he has not done justice, as father he has not restored the family's honor. But the most important function of the two year interval is to give Absalom time to ripen his plans for advancement. He will exact retribution from Amnon only as an initial blow in his coup. Though

Amnon can be killed as part of a personal or family vendetta, the political necessity for Absalom to eliminate the man in front of him is obvious.

For the festival of the shearing of his sheep in Ephraim, Absalom proclaims a celebration for the entire royal family. He invites the King and the whole court to observe it with him. David puts him off, in the face of repeated urging, with the excuse that the expense will be too burdensome for Absalom. David wants no part of any situation where he might find himself in Absalom's power. David may founder as a parent, but when it comes to politics he understands the rules of the game. He is as sensitive to Absalom's true motives as Amnon is unaware. That David would come to the party is too much for Absalom to hope. He never believes that he can get his hands on his father so easily. But now the real objective of the invitation emerges. A fascinating interchange takes place between Absalom and his father (2Sam.13.26): "And shall my brother, Amnon, not come along with me?" We can almost see the innocent look in David's eyes when he asks: "Why should he go with you?" attempting to answer the question with another question. Absalom presses the point, and David consents that Amnon and all the princes of the royal family should attend the celebration.

Why 'all' the sons of the king? Does David hope that there will be some among them who will protect Amnon? He knows that there will be none to raise a finger when surrounded by Absalom's power. It is likely that David desires to avoid the stigma of complicity in the act of vengeance that is to come. If he sends only Amnon with Absalom, people will consider that David was in on the plan or, worse, that the plan was David's and he got Absalom to do the dirty work. This way he is still uninvolved. Moreover, all the other princes will be able to serve as witnesses later on. Unless....

Absalom prepares a feast for all his brothers, but he makes ready a special surprise for one of them. He tells his servants that when Amnon has drunk some wine and is feeling good, the order will be given by Absalom to strike Amnon dead. The ambitious and angry Absalom knows that even his most loyal followers will tremble at the suggestion they murder the crown prince. But Absalom steadies them by taking full responsibility upon himself. He tells them that they should be strong and act like warriors, because they are only obeying orders, his orders. The Bible never actually describes the deed, but simply says that the instructions were carried out. The public assassination of Amnon at the feast of the shearing of the sheep brings about an immediate panic. All of the other princes run for the exits, mount their donkeys, and flee. If the sons of the king are thinking carefully and reasonably about their position, they come to the conclusion that a great struggle for power between David and Absalom is about to take place. It would be important for the princes to hold back to the extent that they can be free later to choose the winning side. But, of course, they are not thinking rationally at this point. Blood has been shed, royal blood like theirs. No one knows how far the bloodshed will go. They have been raised on stories of overdone revenge for rape. They know the accounts of what took place when Dinah was outraged at Shechem. Part of their education has been the history of Israel, including the fate of the Benjaminites after the atrocity at Gibeah. There is little doubt that they were informed about other similar events of which we know nothing.(14) Once Absalom begins to let out the fury he has nurtured for years, who knows where it will stop. Perhaps he has already made the determination that there will be no witnesses to his deed.

In point of fact, the Bible informs us that a report reaches King David immediately. The king, of course, has his spies and representatives at the celebration. His people are probably keeping a twenty-four hour a day watch on Absalom by this time. A messenger departs the scene, probably on horseback, only a moment after Amnon is struck down, in the midst of general panic. It would have been well if the message were delayed for a little while. The word that David receives is a garbled version of the event, and it brings an unnecessary degree of grief to an anxious father. Even while the princes are still on the road back to Jerusalem, the king is told that Absalom has slain all of the king's sons, and not one of them is left. David tears his clothing and throws himself on the ground in grief. His gesture, and in some measure his feelings, are automatically copied by the entire court.

The tale takes an ironic twist at this point. One of the members of the court seems to have a more accurate account of what took place at the festival. Somehow he knows that only one sheep, not the whole flock, has been shorn. This courtier is none other than Jonadab the son of Shimeah, the very same Jonadab, the friend of Amnon without whose incisive advice Amnon might still be alive. Jonadab straightens the king out. He assures David that all the princes are safe, except for one. In an otherwise tight and terse narrative, Jonadab's statement is somewhat wordy (2Sam.13.32-33). "Jonadab son of Shimeah, the brother of David, spoke up to David. He said: 'My lord should not think that all the sons of the king have been killed. Only Amnon is dead. It was at Absalom's order, from the time that his sister was raped. My lord, the king, must pay no attention to the word that all the princes are dead. Amnon is the only one who is dead.'" We are not informed of David's reaction to this. We are left wondering about the subsequent life of the clever Jonadab. It is he who spies the princes coming along the road to Jerusalem and points this out triumphantly to David. But after that, he is never mentioned again in scripture, although at least one writer of fiction has found his character irresistible.(15) Absalom does not return to Jerusalem. He hurries to the safety of the stronghold of his mother's royal family in Geshur in the Golan.

Tamar appears to be forgotten. She may even be dead for all we know. Scripture never mentions her name again. Absalom, however, appears to have genuine feelings of love toward her. He names one of his children after her. So Biblical history records the existence of a third woman of this name. But about this one, the daughter of Absalom, we know nothing more whatsoever.

Those who rail against the supposed male chauvinism of the Biblical world should read the next phase of the account. Absalom languishes at Geshur for years. Then Joab, one of David's most important lieutenants, decides to bring back the man who is now the heir apparent. He cannot approach David with this directly, so he employs a wise woman to carry on the negotiations. She does so with success. Another woman, also characterized as a wise woman, plays an even more important conciliatory role in Second Samuel chapter twenty, verses fourteen through twenty-two. Whenever a delicate situation of life and death had to be negotiated, it seems that these female leaders, known for their diplomacy and respected for their wisdom, were the ones who were called upon. In the introduction we have written a word about the true position of women in scripture and in the Biblical culture. Those who are fair-minded will make an unprejudiced judgement. Perhaps, however, it should once again be pointed out that rape is assessed most harshly in the Biblical scale of values. Amnon is beyond contempt in the eyes of the writers and editors of scripture. Absalom's act of vengeance denies him access to his father's court for a time. But it enhances his standing in the nation at large. It is part of the reason for his rise as a popular figure to such an extent that he is ultimately in a position to challenge David for possession of the throne. In fact, in his revolt, Absalom commands greater forces than the king, holds the city of Jerusalem, and forces David to flee for safety to trans-Jordan. The prince fails in his attempt to seize power only because he listens to bad advice. And, of course, it is the shrewd David who has planted the source of that misleading counsel within the prince's camp. Absalom handles the rape situation with extreme caution, avoiding the excesses that might have doomed him. He prepares his revolt for years, with skill and patience. But he fails for all of that, because his opponent is one of the craftiest political figures in all history.

Chapter VI: FROM BLOOD FEUD TO THE RULE OF LAW

For all of recorded history, the last seven thousand years, and probably for thousands of years before the invention of writing, humanity has edged its way toward the rule of law. We tend to forget that the blood feud is part of the survival pattern of our species. Once human beings began to cling together in families, the members of the group were ready to sacrifice themselves for the sake of their fellow members. We do not know whether this system developed slowly during human evolution or is a natural, genetic endowment. The latter is not unlikely. Bonding in family groups is common among other species of mammals. So the first stage in the evolution of human culture may have come, at least partially, as the result of instinct.

The family bonded as a strong man kept his women to himself as long as he could. Clans and tribes grew from the family. The individual was no longer alone. His or her group was there to offer protection. The men jealously guarded their women. The family, clan, or tribe avenged robbery, kidnapping, rape, or murder by exacting costly punishment from the offending group. The community that sinned was the entity that was punished. Even after laws were promulgated in much of the Near East, the old system of blood feud was not abandoned. People had to be convinced that the new way would work for them. Who would enforce the law? Would it be just and equal for everyone? Could the law protect the poor person or the weak tribe as it did the rich and the strong? Our reading of scripture makes it clear to us that even down into historic times, human beings were ready to have recourse to such force as they could muster when the law failed them or they doubted that it would give them a remedy for their loses. To the Israelites of old, it was plain that if they could not find a way of making the law work reliably, they were bound to suffer repeated catastrophes. The calamity that Shechem son of Hamor brought upon his people or the devastation the lawless ones caused at Gibeah is a reflection of the sort of experience that the human race had endured for a long time. The people wanted a king so that they could have a government based on law, so that individuals rather than groups could be punished.

The Biblical passages we have studied came very, very late in the day for the human race. For more than a thousand years, the Middle East had been moving in the direction of a law code enforced by powerful leaders headed by a king. We tend to think of the code of Hammurabi (Hammurapi is probably a more correct reading of the name) as the first step in the development of our legal system. But Hammurabi's laws were neither original nor were they a code in the proper sense of the word. He drew upon a large body of creative law that was already thousands of years old in his day. Its written origins go back to the Sumerians. Of its pre-historic (pre-writing) roots, we can know nothing. Similar "codes" were forming in other civilizations like China and India at the same time. Only Egypt never evolved a corpus of laws. Each Pharaoh was a law unto himself, erasing, if he wished, any precedents set by his predecessors. None of the bodies of regulations that took shape during this long, long period can really be called a code. They do not have unifying philosophies of law, and they do not cover all aspects of life. Even the earliest collections of Biblical laws, the twenty-first and twenty-second chapters of the book of Exodus, have the character of an agglomeration of case law. These chapters are known as the book of the covenant, but it appears likely that even this "book" represents what is left to us from two old compilations of case law.

They are not very different in style from Hammurabi's code. (We will call it that with reservations, because everyone else does.) But, as we will see, the Biblical legislation represents a culture that has progressed socially and ethically beyond what is reflected in the earlier legal systems. There is no general agreement on Hammurabi's date. He lived, most probably in the first half of the eighteenth century B.C. One educated guess is that Hammurabi reigned in Babylon from 1792-1750 B.C. His legal pronouncements were enshrined in a famous monument, and it is this written record that is responsible for Hammurabi's renown. The monument not only spells out the laws. It portrays the king receiving them from the sun god. We presume that this claim enhances the power of the king and reinforces the authority of the laws. But in a way, Hammurabi is making an admission, also. He is acknowledging the fact that the laws are not original with him and his advisors. We can be sure, however, that the legislation came not from the sun, but from the long historical experience of the peoples of Mesopotamia. The city of Babylon, itself, was an upstart. An older Mesopotamian city was Eshnunna, and it, too, has left us a collection of laws. The code of Eshnunna was ancient in Hammurabi's time. Number twenty-six in the Eshnunna legal list tells us that if a man rapes an engaged girl he is to be killed. The very next provision stipulates that if a girl is seized by a man and carried away without her parents' permission (including that of the mother!) he has no right to keep her. Only if he can make a formal contract with the parents, number twenty-eight tells us, does he have legitimate rights as a husband.(16)

In Hammurabi's code, items 127-184 cover matters to do with sex, engagement, and marriage. Like many other ancient societies, Babylon had sharp class distinctions. There were nobles, government workers and pensioners, ordinary citizens, and slaves. Each of the groups had a different status in the legal system, and the slaves had no rights or protection at all. They were chattel. The full force of the law gave maximum privilege to the members of the nobility. The other groups were subordinate. In Hammurabi's laws, rape was, as at Eshnunna, punishable by death. Again, raping the betrothed girl still living in her father's house (mother may have lost some authority here) was a capital offense.(17) The specific references to the betrothed girl in these codes, and in Biblical law as we shall see, is interesting. Engagement had a binding force far beyond the meaning we give it in our system. The engaged girl had to be protected, and her father indemnified, because her prospective groom was legally her husband. However, he could not cohabit with her until the final arrangements of the marriage contract were completely carried out. This interim period, when the betrothed girl was still living with her parents, put an onerous burden on the father. The law recognized his difficult position and backed him up. In effect, it also guarded the rights of the husband during this awkward period when his honor and social status were vulnerable, but he had no immediate means of preserving them by directly defending his wife from attackers. We probably have a right to assume that the law is so specific in this case because otherwise people could have conjectured about the status of the various individuals involved, especially that of the engaged girl. In other cases of rape, we may assume, the commonly accepted practice of ancient Mesopotamia was to punish rape with death or to look the other way if the fathers, husbands, or brothers of outraged girls took matters into their own hands.

Hittite law reflects a society with different traditions. The Hittites were an Indo-European people who invaded Asia Minor in the second millennium B.C. They built an empire that embraced parts of what is now Turkey, Syria, Lebanon, and Israel. Their legal background was different from the Semitic peoples among whom they lived. Yet there appear to be shared traditions. In a distinct echo of a Biblical law that we will look at soon, the Hittite laws include a provision that if a man rapes a woman in the mountains, he is guilty and is to be killed. But if he rapes her in her house, that is her fault, and both of them may be killed. In this case, the law gives the husband the right to do the killing. But, as in similar cases in the Hammurabi and Eshnunna codes, if he forgives his wife he must also forgive the offending man. (Our emphasis on the question of whether Tamar cried out when Amnon attacked her will become even more meaningful in a little while.) It seems that the Hittite husband had several choices in this case. He could do the killing himself, and with complete impunity. He could forgive both his wife and the adulterer, but not one or the other. Or he could come to the king who would take care of the execution of the woman and the adulterer. The Hittites did not really see him as a rapist if the act took place in the town and the woman did not scream. Hittite life, like that of the Israelites in Bible times, seems to have been more egalitarian that the civilizations of Mesopotamia. There is little or no reference to class privileges in the Hittite laws.(18)

This is not the case when we turn to the laws of Assyria. Tiglath Pileser I, an Assyrian monarch of the twelfth century B.C., left a law code that is generally known as the Middle Assyrian Laws. He lived seven hundred years after Hammurabi, but the code itself may be as much as three hundred years older than Tiglath Pileser I. The Assyrian legal system provides that if a nobleman rapes a noblewoman, he shall die; and she shall be blameless. We are left to assume that if the crime were committed against a woman of lower status, the punishment might be less severe. It is quite likely that the authorities would not take very seriously the rape of a woman of low birth by an aristocrat. Certainly, a slave woman would be fair game for her master. In the spirit of the code, we are safe in assuming that if a noble raped another man's slave, he had better take care not to cause permanent physical injury or he would have to compensate the owner. Numbers 12 through 59 on the list of laws concern matters of sexual relations and marriage. The specific rape law to which we referred is number 12.

The Middle Assyrian Laws also apply the principle of the lex talionis to one type of rape case. Number 55 provides for its application in case a nobleman rapes an unbetrothed virgin. The father of the girl may dispose of the wife of the rapist, taking her or giving her to another man. She need never be returned. In addition, the father is entitled to receive a monetary payment.(19)

Law cannot operate in a vacuum. It is effective in a community only when there is a competent authority to enforce the law. Criminals must be caught, tried, and punished. When the people of ancient Israel demanded a king, they were informed by precisely that perception. They were aware that there were laws. They also knew very well that there was no way to enforce the law. When laws are not enforced, when any phase of the enforcement process breaks down, people find other ways to defend themselves, their possessions, and their values. We have seen through the study of scripture, however (and we know by what is happening in our own society), that when people take the law into their own hands they tend to go too far. They have to go too far. If the tribe punishes another tribe for the crime of an individual, the exacters of punishment have to try to exterminate their foes. If they do not kill them all, a blood feud will develop. Such struggles for honor and security go on and on. The cost in lives becomes immeasurable. This is a principle that operates from the time of Simeon and Levi at Shechem, and enormously long before, to the steps of the courthouse in Welch, West Virginia where the Hatfields and their foes had their final shoot-out, to the gang wars taking place in our big cities today. People would prefer to have a rule of law. But when the law becomes ineffective, they turn the clock of human history back thousands of years and defend themselves in the only way they can.

There was a law in Israel, but there was no authority to enforce it in a dependable fashion. The law codes of the Bible, unlike their predecessors, make no distinctions as to class or social position. Even the king is subject to the law. Even slaves and women captured in battle are protected by it. Resident aliens (think about Lot at Sodom and the old man at Gibeah) are specifically given equality under the law. The earliest strata of Biblical law preserve the injured woman's status as well as the honor and financial interest of her father. The Book of the Covenant in Exodus (Ex.22.15 and 16) confronts the problem of the harm done to both the father and his daughter. One who seduces a virgin must marry her or, if her father refuses the union, the seducer must pay the value of the girl's virginity. As a non-virgin, the girl will now bring a lesser bride price. The seducer must make good the differential in whatever manner the father prescribes. Interestingly enough, the girl seems totally inculpable. When you think about it, this is amazing. Was this girl, of whatever age she may have been, not expected to have some degree of sophistication? Is she utterly innocent because she is incapable of resisting the sweet-talk, the promises, or inducements of some unscrupulous man? From one point of view it is encouraging to find that the law holds her blameless. But, on the other hand, it is somewhat insulting for her to be looked upon as totally irresponsible. It is as if one says to a child: "I'm not surprised at anything you do!"

Centuries later, when the book of Deuteronomy is put together, a different point of view is apparent. The newly married girl whose hymen is not intact is subject to capital punishment. The disgrace she has brought her family must be erased. Although "burnt away" is the Bible's expression, she is killed by stoning. This, and a provision for the execution of both members of a couple caught in an act of adultery are to be found in the twenty-second chapter of Deuteronomy. Verses 14 through 29 state several provisions of the laws regarding sex and marriage. Rape is dealt with specifically in verses 23 to 29. The first of these legal statements (Deut.22.23-4) seems to refer to a case in which a betrothed virgin claims to have been raped in the city, but she did not cry out. The sentence is death for both the man and the maiden, for him because he committed rape and adultery, for her because she did not scream for help. This kind of decision dovetails rather closely with the position of other ancient Middle Eastern law codes on the case, especially with the specifics of the Hittite code.

There can be no doubt that a legal tradition to this effect existed in the time of David. The fact that the book of Deuteronomy was promulgated in the seventh century B.C. does not, by any means, signify that it was totally composed at that time. There are many strata in the book, most of them representing great antiquity. There are certainly numerous ancient traditions that went toward the final product. Only the ultimate editing shows the stamp of a prophetic outlook on Israelite history, morality, and the consequences of Israel's violation of its covenant relationship with God. In the period of David's reign, the importance of considering whether the raped woman screamed would have been taken for granted. David's inaction after Amnon's rape of Tamar is all the more understandable. Suppose we assume that Tamar was an engaged girl. What kind of legal pronouncement can he make under the circumstances? He could condemn both to death. That would satisfy the law and the long-standing tradition. He can pardon both. That will not solve the problem of Tamar's disgrace. So he decides not to decide. The king turns his back on the case and leaves it to Absalom to take the law into his own hands.

We can only sympathize with Tamar's resolution not to cry out. She is not in the same kind of fix as the average woman. She knows that if she shouts no one will come to her aid. If someone hears her at a distance he will not give help in time to prevent the attack. The result of her screaming will not be rescue. It will serve only to publicize her disgrace and make her future life impossible. Whether or not the king and the law deal with Amnon, her own existence will not be an easy one. So she tries, unsuccessfully, to make the best of it. Grasping the provisions of the hallowed law of Israel and its region, we can now understand the depths of her dilemma and some of the ramifications of the case. But what if Tamar is not engaged? We will look at the possible disposition of that case in a moment.

The betrothed girl is blameless if the rape took place in the field, out of earshot of any settled area. It cannot be emphasized too strongly that in this case the woman's word is taken over that of the man in a capital offense. There is a double assumption to be made on the part of judges in Bible times. Both assumptions are in favor of the female. We assume that she is the one who is telling the truth, and there is no demand whatsoever for corroborative evidence. We also assume that she did cry out. She does not even have to make a claim to that effect. To the credit of the society and civilization involved, we have to take notice that there was one further assumption. They took it as an absolute that if a woman under attack did scream for help, people would come running to save her. It would seem that in three or four thousand years we have progressed in the wrong direction.

The last of the series of laws in this category can serve to give us a glimpse into a view of life very different from our own. We already know that in Biblical law as well as in the legal systems of parallel cultures, adulterers and rapists were subject to capital punishment. But the end of Deuteronomy's chapter twenty-two (Deut.22.28-29) makes us realize that when it comes to comprehending alien civilizations we do not always understand what we think we understand. Apparently, it is not the act of rape, in and of itself, that causes the rapist to be condemned to death. A major part of his guilt lies in the fact that it is a formally engaged or married woman that he attacked. These last two verses of the chapter throw a curve at us. They provide that if a man rapes an uncommitted virgin, he must pay the father of the girl a reduced bride price and marry his victim. What is more, he may never divorce her; this in a society where divorce, though uncommon as far as we know, was extremely easy. We realize right away that we are in a world very different from our own. The law intends to protect those whom it considers the injured parties. The father is partially compensated for his loss of the full bridal price. (And we must remember that the payment of a bridal price to a father was compensation for the loss of an asset, the contribution his daughter made toward the prosperity of his household.) The woman is "reimbursed," in their eyes at least, for the loss of status she has suffered. Now, from their point of view, her status is restored because she becomes a married woman. Even more, she is in a stronger position than other women for her whole life because her husband can never divorce her. But from our viewpoint there are questions. Suppose she does not like the idea of being married to the ruffian who has manhandled her? He probably has little affection for her, and he does not really seem like an ideal husband. How can such a marriage, even if it turns out to be workable, serve to repay her for the physical and mental pain she has endured? Won't there be just a shadow of doubt in people's minds in most cases of this type that she might not have told the truth, she or her father might have faked the rape, she might have made a false accusation just to nail a husband, etc? We can see these suspicions following her in the mouths of the village gossips for the rest of her days. It is likely that the old lawmakers also thought of these problems. They could answer us that this is not an ideal world, and they are just trying to make the best of a bad situation. If they leave the girl stranded, she will never get married. Her shame will cling to her forever, and through no fault of her own. This way we give her a chance for a decent life and hope that it will all come out reasonably well.

Now, to belabor the Amnon-Tamar case once more, we fully appreciate the stone wall that David faced. Suppose Tamar is not engaged. He cannot force marriage upon them because it would be incestuous. The legal tradition does not contemplate such a case. True, Amnon violates the principle set forth in Leviticus (Lev.18.11). But Leviticus provides for no individual punishment for such an infraction against the laws of incest and consanguinity. It is not clear that Leviticus eighteen is law in the usual sense of the term. From the way this chapter in Leviticus is written, we have to conclude that sexual misconduct and incest bring disaster upon the entire community, but not necessarily in the lifetime of the guilty parties. It is not clear what, if any, direct punishment can be administered to the guilty individuals. So if Tamar is not engaged, David is left to make a law where none exists or to punish his son outside the law. He cannot bring himself to do either.

Jacob's confrontation with the ruler of Shechem is more problematic than the issue faced by King David. At David's time, in the mind of the Biblical writer, the laws of the Torah have long been in possession of the people of Israel. The doctrine already existed that the Torah was given through Moses to Israel. David would be expected, if possible, to administer justice according to the law. Jacob, on the other hand, lived in a time before the giving of the law. That puts him in another category. In the eyes of the Biblical writer, editor, or reader; Jacob is not expected to live by a law that has not yet been given. Jacob and the other patriarchs do a great many things that would violate the Torah. Abraham marries his own half-sister. Jacob marries two full sisters. He buries the pagan idols instead of grinding and burning them. He is embalmed, as is Joseph, after death. His grandfather, Abraham, serves milk and meat together to visitors. Later on, Moses or his son is circumcised by a woman. All these events are a few examples of the many actions reported in the Torah that are against the later laws of the Torah. The editors of the text were liberal enough to leave these strong traditions in place.

But in light of what we know about the existence of a great body of law and tradition common throughout the region, Jacob is aware that there is provision for the problem he faces with his daughter Dinah and Shechem son of Hamor. The prince has raped Dinah, an unengaged girl. As an aristocrat and a member of the ruling people of the area, he might expect to go off free. But he wants the girl for a wife. When he and his father come to Jacob and the brothers of the girl, Shechem knows that he can be required to pay at least a part of the bride price for her. He is ready to be generous. He asks the men to name any price, and he will pay it. If the traditions we have discussed are, as we think, already long in place; he anticipates no serious impediments. Jacob may feel that way too. But then Simeon and Levi take action and kill all the members of the community that they feel has dishonored their sister and their family. Having examined the old laws and traditions, we can now understand more fully why Jacob departs so hastily from the scene. His boys have not obeyed the norms. They have not acted within the boundaries of proper behavior. That is why the father feels so vulnerable.

Before we leave the subject of the ancient laws, we should point out one additional feature. It reflects well on their view of women and badly on ours. Nowhere in any of the ancient law codes, and the ones we have looked at cover a period of around 1500 years, is there the slightest hint of an attempt to blame the victim for the fact that a rape occurred. We see not a single word about provocative dress or behavior. At least in the Hittite and scriptural laws the relative social standing of the woman and the man are of no consequence. In the Bible's system, difference of race or nationality would not affect the principle of equal justice for all parties. The fact that the girl is alone out in the field (or in Hittite law on the mountain) has no special significance and does not serve to soften the accusation against the criminal. It is only in late classical times and in the early Middle Ages that the idea dawns upon men that they can put the blame for the very rape itself on the woman. To our shame, this thinking still pops up at times in our own courts of law today. Again, we have to say, we seem to have progressed backwards.

By the time of Deuteronomy, one can speak about the beginning of the formation of a truly comprehensive law code. After the fifth century B.C., in a Judea restored after the Babylonian exile, such a code grew and took shape. It was not finally codified until the middle of the second century A.D. At that time, under the pressure of Roman oppression, a thoroughly systematic legal work, the Mishneh, was edited and published. In subsequent centuries, in both Babylonia and the Land of Israel, it was exquisitely elaborated in profound casuistic ramification and eventually published in two collections: the Palestinian Talmud in the fourth century A.D. and the Babylonian Talmud (the work most people mean when they say 'the' Talmud) in the sixth century. Those tomes, and the codifications of Jewish law that were made during the Middle Ages, have a good deal to say on our subject.(20)

Not only in post-Biblical Jewish life, but throughout a great many human cultures and civilizations, a still higher level of social order was reached. Beyond law, there arose the concept of status and civil rights.

To contemplate the process by which this came about, we can review the stages in simple terms. For this purpose, let us get away from the rape theme for a moment. We can take for an example the issue of assault. At the earliest, or most rudimentary level, let us say that a man hits me on the nose. I do not like being hit on the nose, so I hit him back; harder, if possible, than he hit me. But suppose I am unable to defend myself. He is bigger or stronger than I am. Or he runs so fast that I cannot catch him. In that case, I ask my brothers to help out. Together we confront the culprit and beat him up. Justice has been done, but there is, of course, more to come. He returns with his whole family, and a gang fight ensues. After several more plateaux of escalation are reached, there are three dead, twelve seriously injured, and the rest of us have a pretty good headache.

Sooner or later, we all conclude that there must be a better way. The two tribes meet and forgive one another. We decide that from now on we will punish people for their wrongs on an individual basis. We have invented the idea of law. The next time that bully punches me in the nose, the chief of his own group will judge him. If found guilty, the criminal will be punished. Each wrong committed within or between the tribes will be handled case by case. The miscreants will be given suitable retribution, suffering the same pain and damage which they inflicted on someone else.

That'll teach 'em. They'll think twice before trying that again! But there is one trouble, still. My nose is broken. It does not hurt any less or look any straighter than it did before they broke my attacker's nose. The tribes meet again (hundreds or thousands of years later, of course) and arrive at a new idea. Whenever a case of damages comes up, the chiefs will decide not only on punishment for the perpetrator, but will also level a material fine. The politicians will certainly take a part of that payment. But the rest will go to fix the damage, or at least make me feel better about my broken nose.

This marks a new stage of creative law. Now, every time there is an injury, the leaders find a remedy through payment of cash or kind. But, at this point, the law begins to become less and less creative. The same cases and types of cases arise over and over again. Everyone knows that a broken nose is worth four sheep or eight pieces of silver, one-fourth to the judges, three-fourths to the victim. The law is being codified. Even entirely new cases can be handled in the spirit of what has already been worked out. If the nose is worth four sheep, and it does not keep the injured party from hunting or working, then a broken leg is worth ten sheep, plus six weeks of food for the victim and his dependents. We are arriving at a code of laws that can deal not only with cases as they appear before the court but can also anticipate new cases before they happen. This "what if" stage of law deals not only in contingencies, but subtleties. The broken nose means more to the witch doctor or story teller, who must appear and speak in public, than to the hunter or tool maker.

Further complications occur with the rise of social inequalities. Just try breaking the nose of the son of the chief! The law recognizes various classes and offers greater protection to the rich and powerful than to the poor and lowly. Royalty and nobility, aristocracy and the very wealthy, common citizens, military veterans, retired government workers, and the native poor all have different status within the law. At the bottom of the scale are the slaves and the aliens, people with no visible legal shield whatsoever. Ancient Hebrew law, to its glory, was one of the few codes of antiquity to offer equal protection under the statutes to all, from the king to the slaves and aliens. Perhaps it was the only code to reach this height.

It is not easy for us to appreciate the kind of law code created by most of the peoples of the classical and the medieval world. In Europe, the Arab empires, India, and the Far East; the class affiliation of the victim and the perpetrator determined the seriousness of the punishment. If the king broke your nose, there was not much you could do. If you broke the king's nose, you would be lucky if you could run for your life. Yet the feudal system, in its way, was progressive. It paved the path to a higher legal concept. The various classes learned their places. That not only kept them where they belonged in the legal scheme of things. It gradually gave each of them a strong sense of the protection and status that were their due. The nobles, in particular, fought hard to preserve their position in relationship to the king. What had come into being was a concept of 'rights'. From the Shogunate in Japan, to the Fronde in France and the Magna Carta in England; the nobles struggled toward this concept, and gave it to the world. It remained only for the other classes, too, to claim their own rights. And then, in a later time, it was possible for the idea of equal rights for all human beings to be born. The Declaration of Independence in America and the "Rights of Man" in revolutionary France embodied this new plateau in human development.

What the signers of the Declaration of Independence really meant by "all men are created equal" is not easy for us to know. But, in a sense, it is immaterial. "Men" may have signified "white, Protestant, free males who own property" when the Declaration was first written. If so, that makes no differences whatsoever now. Long ago, the whole world came to understand that the message was that everyone of whatever race, creed, color, nationality, social standing, or gender shares equal status before the law and has the right to equal treatment and protection. The man who punches me in the nose, then, not only causes me pain and injury for which he must be punished and made to pay compensation. He violates my civil rights, my status as a citizen and human being.

But the idea of civil rights takes the matter a step further. Certainly, the law itself is concerned with more than individuals. The tranquility and stability of society depend on the fair administration of justice. Things come apart very rapidly, as we have said and seen, when justice is absent or fails. The principle of civil rights reaches still deeper. The very order of things is upset by the violation of people's rights. When I am down with that broken nose, I can no longer do my duty or exercise all my rights or fulfill many of my obligations as a citizen. I am not the only one deprived. The entire community is unalterably and irreparably harmed. Because I have been deprived of my rights, the entire constitutional system is threatened.

It is not so difficult to apply these concepts to the issue of rape. Every human being, woman and man, has the right, automatically, to be secure in his or her person. We all have the right to pursue happiness. But your right to swing your arm ends where my nose begins. A man's right to sexual satisfaction ends where a woman's noes begin.

Every person, women and men, have the inherent right to determine who shall and shall not touch them, and when. Placing rape in the realm of civil rights conveys great advantages in social control. It places the crime on a new, higher and more effective, legal level. Violation of civil rights implies constitutional involvement. It puts the matter at a federal height of interest. Thus, if civil rights are involved, the pressure on the rapist grows greater. Also, compensation to the victim can be claimed more insistently. It is entirely desirable that this step be established legally. It will be most useful if the public mind can absorb the concept that a sexual assault on a woman is an attack against the total fabric of constitutional rights under which we are all protected.

CONCLUSION

It would be nice to think that we have solved something. We probably have not. The terror of rape will loom over our lives along with other crimes of violence. No book is going to change that. Vigilante counter-violence did not end it in ancient times. It will not do so today. Laws succeeded in controlling it in the past only to a certain extent. That condition will likely remain more or less the same.

Still, perhaps by small degrees, we humans are capable of learning to behave sanely. Men can be taught to see women as persons first, although we will probably go on seeing them also as sexual objectives. They see us that way too. Men can certainly learn to stop trying to blame women for rape. There is a sharp-barbed story that comes to mind in this connection. In the early days of the Zionist movement, Jewish Palestine was composed of idealists and utopians. Crimes of violence, including sexual assault, were all but unknown within the Jewish community. Then, as a broader sampling of European and Middle Eastern Jews flowed into the country during the thirties, the population became "normalized" to an extent. At some point, there was a rash of rapes in Jerusalem. The Jewish council met in a spirit of deep concern. One of the wise men on the group proposed that a curfew be placed on women. That would keep them home and prevent the assaults. At that point, Golda Meir, later to be prime minister of Israel, rose to speak to the effect that since it was men who were committing these crimes, the curfew should be put on them, not on the women. It was a point well taken, and one that many men still have not learned to understand.

Rosy-eyed pessimism would be a way to characterize our views. Humans are capable of progress. Behavior can be modified. But change comes so slowly in some things that we begin to despair. However, when women stand up strongly for their rights, and men of good will pay proper attention to the issue, the writer is convinced that there can be improvement.

Another objective of our writing this book was to bring out a fair view of the Bible. We will not use the term "objective," for no one can achieve that. The Bible is too many things to too many people. It is hopeless to think that we can ever reach a purely critical, historical appreciation of the Bible. It represents a distant time, a different culture, an alien world. So does all ancient literature. But in addition to that, the Bible is seen through the eyes of many varying traditions. It is an object of faith, conviction, rejection, contempt, misunderstanding, mistranslation, misreading, and malice.

But at least we have set the record straight in keeping with the best of our own lights. Some feminist writers seem bent on broadening misunderstanding. One author, for example, has written a book on rape which is, for the most part, a very useful survey. But, as part of a historical section, her assumptions about the Bible add up to: Since it was written by men, Jewish men in particular, it must be a work of male chauvinism.(21) She sets out to prove these axioms to her own satisfaction. But nowhere can she bring herself to admit the plain fact about the Bible's overall position. She simply cannot admit that in the Biblical scale of values, in both narrative and law, rape is rejected; is something "just not done." She is not alone in failing to recognize that the Biblical world was conflicted in its view on women, just like all other cultures, down to our own day. It seems hard for some people to accept the clear truth that substantial parts of the Hebrew scriptures, perhaps more that we realize, were composed by women.

It would be a super-human task to set out to correct all misconceptions about the Bible, all prejudices that men have about women, all resentments that women feel against men, all existing misunderstanding that religious groups harbor toward one another. The main purposes of this particular little book have been 1) to add a voice of protest against the violence that threatens women and 2) to clarify the Bible's position on the subject; in other words to increase understanding in two directions.

Some of the worst advice that can be given to speakers and writers is to "tell 'em what you're gonna say, say it, and then tell 'em what you said." If we have said it plainly once within the body of this work, that will suffice.

BIBLIOGRAPHY

Aharoni, Yohanan and Avi-Yonah, Michael. The Macmillan Bible Atlas. New York - London 1968

Anchor Bible, The. Garden City various dates

Boling, Robert G. Judges
McCarter, Jr., P. Kyle. Second Samuel Speiser, E.A. Genesis

Brownmiller, Susan. Against Our Will: Men, Women and Rape. Toronto et al. 1975

Bulfinch's Mythology. New York 1989

The Complete Greek Tragedies vol.III Euripides.

David Grene and Richmond Lattimore, eds. Chicago 1955

Encyclopaedia Judaica. Jerusalem 1972

Epstein, Louis M. Sex Laws and Customs in Judaism. New York 1948

Harsh, Philip Whaley. A Handbook of Classical Drama. Stanford 1944

Hebrew Bible (Massoretic Text). ed. Letteris. Berlin 1937

Holy Bible, The. The Revised Berekely Version. Nashville 1982

Holy Bible, The. Revised Standard Version. Toronto, etc. 1952

Holy Scriptures, The. Jewish Publication Society. Phila. 1952

Gager, Nancy and Schurr, Cathleen. Sexual Assault: Confronting Rape in America. New York 1976

Jacobson, Dan. The Rape of Tamar. New York 1970

Mandelkern, Solomon. Veteris Testamenti Concordantiae. Leipzig 1925

Pritchard, James B. Ancient Near Eastern Texts Relating to the Old Testament. 2nd ed. Princeton 1955

Racine, Jean. Phaedra. translation by Wesley Goddard. San Francisco 1961

Strong, James. The New Strong's Concordance of the Bible. Nashville 1985

NOTES

1. We are translating "rape" here in Gen.34.2 with Speiser in the Anchor Bible Genesis. But Jewish Publication Society (J.P.S.) and The Revised Standard Version (R.S.V.) have "humbled." and others like The Revised Berkeley Version have "dishonored." If "rape" is not the true meaning of the word used in the Hebrew text, this passage does not warrant the place of a separate chapter in the present work. The most common word for rape in later Hebrew is 'anas.' But dictionaries also give the word 'ina,' the word used in the chapter under consideration. In fact, the meanings offered, like "humbled" or "dishonored," are completely unjustified. (Although if "dishonored" is meant to be a euphemism for "rape," we should accept it.) The root meaning of 'ina' is "to hurt." By extension, in Biblical Hebrew, it was used to express "to torture," "to oppress," "to afflict;" "to rape," "to violate," and "to force." 'Ina' is, in fact, the common Biblical word for rape. It is used in that sense, incontrovertibly, in Deuteronomy twenty-two and in Second Samuel thirteen. Gen.34.2 is seldom well translated. "He took her and lay with her and raped her." will simply not do. It ignores the spirit of the ancient Hebrew language where groups of two or more words, in this case verbs, are strung together to convey a single thought. The correct meaning expressed in English the way we would speak or write it is something like "he grabbed her to lie with her forcibly." In plain talk, he raped her. It may very well be that it was from the wording of this account that the word 'ina' first began to take on the meaning of "rape" in Biblical Hebrew, and the original meaning of Gen.34.2 was "he took her to bed inflicting pain."

2. It is possibly the meaning of Israel in Gen.49.28, although the use of the word "tribes" makes it less likely. Altogether, we have to think that the name was not used in this sense. If it means extended family or clan, or the like, in Gen.34, we would have to consider it unique there. That makes it all the more probable that we are dealing with an expression supplied later, under the pressure of different political needs.
3. Hebrew 'betah' gives the feeling "with a sense of security." The translations give "unawares" (Revised standard Version and J.P.S.) and "unopposed" (Anchor Bible Genesis). Elsewhere in scripture, the word 'betah,' is used in the sense of "secure" or safe; cf.Deut.12.10; 33.28; Ju.8.11;1Sam.12.11. But Ezek.30.9 may be close to the meaning we use here, i.e., "with ease." But the English translations miss the point.
4. The translations generally treat the text otherwise. Anchor Bible Genesis has "And should our sister have been treated like a whore?" Revised Standard Version reads "Should he treat our sister like a whore?" J.P.S. translates "Should one deal with our sister as with a harlot?" All we can say is that our own translation is close to the literal meaning of the very simple Hebrew words. Linguistics aside, Shechem does not treat Dinah like a prostitute (the way that Judah deals with Tamar). Shechem rapes Dinah. When he is through with her, men might consider her good for nothing better than prostitution. He ruins her in the eyes of her brothers. Quite simply, from a masculine point of view at that time, and not just at that time, he has rendered her so that she can never be a respectable woman. Linguistically and logically our translation makes sense.

5. Quotes and references, as well as the general line of "The Story of the Two Brothers" are taken from James B. Pritchard, ed. The Ancient Near East. vol.I. An Anthology of Texts and Pictures. Princeton 1958. pp.12-16.
6. The phrases in Gen.39.17, "came to me to sport with me" are handled in a variety of ways by the translations. Revised Standard Version has "came in to me to insult me." Jewish Publication Society has "came unto me to mock me." More imaginatively, Berkeley has "came to my room to molest me." There are two elements here.

   The phrase "ba elay" is hardly a problem. "Came to me" suffices. The fact that "ba" may mean "to enter" would have no special significance here. The drift of the meaning is "he approached me" in both senses, coming near and making a proposition.

   The problem is the words "l'tsakhek bi". It would have been pleasing to be able to translate something like "to have his pleasure with me." But that translation would be difficult to justify (although it is possibly correct). The use of the word in Exodus 32.6 is probably sexual in tone. But that meaning hardly fits the context of Judges 16.25. Under the circumstances, one resorts to vague translations and double meanings such as "to fool around" in the golden calf passage in Exodus and "sport with me" in our text in Genesis.

   We should resent it, however, when the translators, though recognizing the sexual character of the text (and it does not take a Sherlock Holmes to detect it in Gen.39), give us these bowdlerized interpretations. Perhaps we should let Berkeley off the hook with its "molest."
7. The king was to be anointed by the priest, therefor, in effect, by God. Thus the king became the "anointed of

the Lord." In Hebrew that reads "m'shiakh Yahveh." "Mashiakh" (the absolute form of the construct "M'shiakh") is the word which becomes "messiah" in English. It means the "anointed one" and is short for "anointed of the Lord." The messiah, in Jewish tradition, will be a descendant of King David. He will be the true king of Israel.

When Christians came to translate the term into Greek, they used the Greek word for "anointed one" or "christos," that is Christ. So the very name of the religion, Christianity, comes out of the fierce process by which ancient Israel decided to try and be like the other nations and have a king of its own. Judaism, and even more so Christianity, was formed out of that decision. The theological conviction on which the decision was based was that God does not, or cannot, save all by himself. He must, therefor, send an anointed one–messiah–christ as rescuer–savior. It might be considered a strange decision for a people that had experienced salvation at the Red Sea to have made. But it was the one they made.

8. In Ju.19.18 there is an important question to settle. It has little or nothing to do with our subject of rape. But it is vital for the dating of the story as well as for understanding the history of the development of the Levitical priesthood. The Levite tells the old man that he is going home to the edge of the hill country of Ephraim. He adds, according to the Masoretic Hebrew text (the text in common usage) that he is going to the "house of the Lord," or the "house of Yahveh." Ancient versions of the scripture, however, have "my house." These ancient translators, especially the Jews who translated the Bible into Greek, were extremely careful of their language and interpretation. To them it was the most sacred of texts, and they never took

liberties with it. This means that the translator here was working from a different, or variant, Hebrew text.

There are several possible explanations for the divergence in readings. 1) An out and out error in copying was made somewhere along the line. The Septuagint (Greek Jewish) translators had one version, and our Masoretic text retained the other. 2) A scribe, at some point in time, mistook the Hebrew letter yod (the letter "Y") at the end of the word 'beti' = "my house" as an abbreviation for the name of God. That scribe decided to write it out in full. This would account for the reading in our common text. 3) More exciting, an editor at a time when the Levites had become the religious leaders of the Israelite community, tried to read back the priestly functions onto an earlier period. Anachronistically, he invests the Levite with a role that his tribe had still not begun to play. This editor reasoned that if the Levite was going back to his area of residence, it must be to serve as a priest. Therefor, it would be natural for him to say that he was returning to God's house. That would be more important than the mere, obvious fact that he was going to his own human habitation.

9. We are translating the famous 'b'nay b'liya-al' as "lawless persons." The Hebrew word, often rendered "belial," with or without a capital "B," has a rich cultural history. In post-Biblical times, it came to serve as a proper name, a synonym for Satan. Literally, the word might appear to be a compound of two Hebrew words meaning "without use," "useless." The idea that there might have been a band of homosexuals that was given this name because they would have been unlikely to sire children is far-fetched, and smacks of low prejudice at high scholarly levels.

In fact, the derivation is not quite clear. Compound words are not in the spirit of the Hebrew language. They are almost unheard of in Biblical Hebrew. The word is used in various settings no less than twenty-six times in the Hebrew Bible. It is invariably pejorative. The meanings range across the ideas of "disruptive" and "riotous" to "light-headed," "irreverent," "faithless," "disrespectful," "dishonest," "false" (as of a witness), "hostile," and "misleading." There is no parallel in any of the word's occurrences to the level of hideous violence displayed by the people in the passage under consideration. A good review of the usage and history of the word may be found in the brief notice in the Encyclopaedia Judaica, vol.4, p.427, col.2f.

10. As startling as the Levite's method of propagandizing may seem to us, it is, as we have indicated, not wholly original. He drew upon a traditional system of spreading the word. In First Samuel (1Sam.11.7), Saul dismembers a bull for a similar purpose. The prophet Ahijah cuts a garment in twelve parts to dramatize the division of the kingdom under Rehoboam (1Ki.11.29ff.). There is an interesting note on page 276 of Anchor Bible to Judges.
11. Many Bible atlases provide excellent maps and descriptions of the battle for Gibeah. See, for instance, the Macmillan Bible Atlas, p.81.
12. For a general discussion of the subject of the condemned city, see Talmud Bavli Sanhedrin beginning with the long Mishnah that starts on 111b and the gemara that runs on to 112a.
13. The Hebrew word for the food being prepared is 'l'vivot'. It is possibly related to the Hebrew word for heart, 'levav.' For an interesting discussion of the erotic puns that may exist in this connection, especially

in Amnon's statement to David, see the Anchor Bible to II Samuel, p.322, the note to verse 6.

14. The author's point of view about the Bible is covered in the introduction. It is our feeling that educated young people during the beginning of the first millenium B.C. would have been exposed to a large selection of literature. They would have had a sizeable library at hand, covering a multitude of what we would call secular and religious subjects.
15. The Rape of Tamar by Dan Jacobson is a novel in which the entire history is seen through the eyes of Jonadab. The heavy- handed anachronisms in this work of fiction are probably intentional and may be intended as humorous or ironic. Unavoidably, Jacobson attempts to clarify the course of events by psychological and psychoanalytic speculation. The result is not wholly convincing.
16. This and other references to the ancient legal codes are taken from Pritchard, "Ancient Near Eastern Texts Relating to the Old Testament" (abbreviated as ANET). For the laws of Eshnunna, see page 162, ##26-28.
17. See ANET p.171, #130.
18. For the Hittite laws, see ANET, especially #197 on p.196.
19. The provision of the death penalty is in ANET p.181, #12. The case of the uncommitted virgin is on p.185, #55.
20. For a sketch that will indicate the scope and dimensions of rabbinic law on the subject of rape, see Epstein. Sex Laws and customs in Judaism, ch.8, pp.183ff. Epstein also has a very, very brief section on Biblical legislation in the same chapter, see pp.179ff.
21. See Susan Brownmuller. Against our Will: Men, Women and Rape. The main discussion on the Bible is in pp.9-14.

ABOUT THE AUTHOR

The author of ***Rape and the Bible***, **Alton Meyer Winters**, is a lifelong student of the Bible and the languages in which it is written. For many years he was a translator and interpreter. His knowledge covers French, German, and Russian as well as Hebrew and Aramaic. In addition to translations published from modern Hebrew works, he recently authored a homiletic study: ***Stories of the Dubner Maggid***.

This author grew up in Baltimore and studied at Johns Hopkins University and the University of Cincinnati. Winters was ordained at the Hebrew Union College in Cincinnati in 1947. He cultivated literary and linguistic interests even while he served in the pulpit until retirement.

Rape and the Bible reflects Rabbi Winters's long commitment to women's rights and feminism. For many years he was involved in Planned Parenthood and Family Service organizations. In the book, he seeks to demonstrate that we have still not caught up with the Bible's standards in dealing with the problem of rape.

www.ingramcontent.com/pod-product-compliance
Ingram Content Group UK Ltd.
Pitfield, Milton Keynes, MK11 3LW, UK
UKHW040601210726
13854UKWH00008B/1666

9 781588 203250